PUBLIC SERVICE AND DEMOCRACY:
Ethical Imperatives for the 21st Century

Migrant Mother
Nipomo, California, March 1936, by Dorothea Lange
(*Courtesy of the Library of Congress*)

Public Service

and

Democracy

Ethical Imperatives for the 21st Century

Louis C. Gawthrop
University of Baltimore

CHATHAM HOUSE PUBLISHERS

SEVEN BRIDGES PRESS, LLC

NEW YORK • LONDON

Public Service and Democracy:
Ethical Imperatives for the 21st Century

SEVEN BRIDGES PRESS, LLC
P.O. BOX 958, CHAPPAQUA, NEW YORK 10514-0958

PUBLISHER: Robert J. Gormley
COVER DESIGN: Inari Information Services, Inc.
MANAGING EDITOR: Katharine Miller
PRODUCTION SUPERVISOR: Melissa A. Martin
COMPOSITION: Bang, Motley, Olufsen
PRINTING AND BINDING: Versa Press, Inc.

LIBRARY OF CONGRESS CATALOGING-IN-PUBLICATION DATA
  Gawthrop, Louis C.
    Public service and democracy : ethical imperatives
      for the 21st century / Louis C. Gawthrop
        p. cm.
    Includes bibliographical references and index.
    ISBN 1-56643-070-4 (pbk.)
    ISBN 1-56643-075-5 (cloth)
      1. Bureaucracy—United States. 2. Democracy—United
  States. 3. Political ethics—United States. I. Title.
  JK421 .G37   1998
  351.73—ddc21   98-25377
                                                     CIP

Manufactured in the United States of America
10   9   8   7   6   5   4   3   2   1

To V.B.G.

*Whose presence is reflected
in all that is fitting*

Now this is not the end. It is not even the beginning of the end. But it is perhaps, the end of the beginning.

— Winston Churchill,
November 1942

In the end, as in the beginning, we are responsible to each other and for each other. It is that kind of island, the earth.

— James Carroll,
National Catholic Reporter,
23 June 1972

Contents

Introduction

IN TWO recent and influential books that aim to improve the commonweal, both concerned primarily with "reinventing government," the notion of entrepreneurship is paramount. The subtitle of David Osborne and Ted Gaebler's book, *Reinventing Government*, is *How the Entrepreneurial Spirit Is Transforming the Public Sector from Schoolhouse to Statehouse, City Hall to the Pentagon*; the subtitle of a companion volume by David Osborne and Peter Plastrik, *Banishing Bureaucracy*, is more succinct: *The Five Strategies for Reinventing Government*.[1]

The key words usually attached to the meaning of entrepreneurship are business, management, initiative, innovation, creativity, and risk. These terms supply some of the emotive connotations that are absent from the rather sterile definition supplied by Osborne and Gaebler in *Reinventing Government*: the shift of "economic resources out of an area of lower yield and into an area of higher productivity and greater yield." By contrast, Osborne and Plastrik, in *Banishing Bureaucracy*, provide a more expansive definition:

> Reinvention is about replacing bureaucratic systems with entrepreneurial systems. It is about creating public organizations and systems that habitually innovate, that continually improve their quality, without having to be pushed from outside. It is creating a public sector that has a built-in desire to improve.[2]

As I discuss in the latter part of chapter 1, the arguments advanced in these two books are not particularly novel. What is new about them, however, is the appropriateness of Osborne and

Gaebler's subtitle: *How the Entrepreneurial Spirit Is Transforming the Public Sector from Schoolhouse to Statehouse, City Hall to the Pentagon.* At the present time across our nation, major efforts are being exerted and significant resources are being expended—from the schoolhouse to the statehouse, and, indeed, to the White House; from city halls to the halls of Congress—in an attempt to infuse the spirit of entrepreneurship into public-sector organizations.

Many of the underlying premises contained in *Reinventing Government* and *Banishing Bureaucracy* are reflected in the chapters of this book. The principal focus of this volume, however, is on the ethical-moral values and virtues that pervade the spirit of democracy and constitute the pathways to the common good. The core argument advanced is that these values and virtues must function as guideposts and benchmarks for those who serve in the name of democracy. The democratic spirit and the entrepreneurial spirit are, by no means, antithetical concepts; indeed, many of the implicit values embedded in the current reinventing government literature also constitute the essence of our democratic spirit. The underlying thesis of this book, however, is that the value vision of democracy must serve as the lifeblood of the entrepreneurial spirit if the current efforts at reinventing government are to prevail. Otherwise, we are left with another set of misused and misdirected management pronouncements in our never-ending quest to shape public-sector organizations into viable systems capable of moving us closer to the democratic vision of the common good.

Chapter 1 is primarily descriptive in that it provides an overarching (albeit highly compressed) framework that tracks the development of public-sector bureaucracy in our unique democratic system of governance. The subsequent chapters provide an in-depth focus on specific concepts associated with this development that are fundamentally related to the spirit of democracy as envisioned at the birth of our new Republic. Thus, chapter 2 speaks to the contradictory dynamics that energize democracy and bureaucracy and the manner in which the fault lines that mark this terrain are frequently covered over with the cloak of hypocrisy. Chapter 3 considers the historical development of public administration since the founding of the Republic and the manner in which the elements of bureaucracy have been configured to fit in the essence of the American character. Chapter 4 focuses on the notion of public service and what it means in our system of governance to serve in the spirit of democracy. Chapter 5 presents a quasi case study by demonstrating how the entrepreneurial spirit, dramatically evidenced during the New Deal days, was energized and made manifest by an unabashed commitment to the common good. The notion of the common good is carried over to chapter 6, where its relevance to our bureaucratic-democratic ethos is discussed in broader, more inclusive terms. Finally, in chapter 7, a theme that winds its way through the previous chapters is addressed directly. In this final chapter it is argued that public-sector ethics is vacuous and the dynamic engine of democracy is stalled unless a moral connection is made between democracy and bureaucracy. That is to say, the ethos of public service, so essential for the spirit of democracy to flourish, can be realized only if directed by a moral imperative bound to the common good.

I

Rediscovering Democracy — Is Anybody Listening?

IN THE early years of the formation of our Republic—that is, the period from 1789 to 1829, covering the presidency of George Washington through that of John Quincy Adams—the relationship that evolved in the United States between the art of governing a democratic polity and the craft of managing the specifics associated with such governance was relatively well synchronized. In those initial, formative years of America's grand experiment, there was virtually no discernible distinction between the policymakers and the policy implementers, at least insofar as their shared perceptions of a purposeful sense of mission were concerned. Those associated with the new government, regardless of their role or position, reflected, for the most part, a deeply embedded sense of commitment to the transcendent promise of democracy—the Good Society—as well as a deeply embedded sense of moral responsibility for the well-being of their fellow citizens. The tone and temper set by George Washington at the outset of his first administration were not far removed from the sentiments expressed a century and a half earlier by the proprietary founder and Royal Governor of the Massachusetts Bay Colony, John Winthrop, to his followers as they prepared to land in Massachusetts:

> We must strengthen, defend, preserve, and comfort each other. We must love one another, we must bear one another's burdens. We must look not only on our things, but also on the things of our brethren. We must rejoice together, mourn together, labor and suffer together.[1]

To be sure, the mindsets and worldviews of the early Puritans and the Founding Fathers were poles apart. Nevertheless, the general population of the thirteen original states knew exactly what was meant when the Framers of the Constitution stated in its Preamble:

> We the people of the United States, in order to form a more perfect union, establish justice, insure domestic tranquility, provide for the common defense, promote the general welfare, and secure the blessings of liberty to ourselves and our posterity, do ordain and establish this Constitution for the United States of America.

If the early Puritans viewed themselves as embarking on a divine mission, guided by the hand of God, the citizens of the new Republic were engaged in a much more practical and secular undertaking: how to create a representative democracy in which ultimate responsibility for the success or failure of the undertaking would depend on each individual's willingness to acknowledge the mutual dependency between personal self-interests and the common good. Of course, the basic democratic values of individual freedom and justice were the driving forces that energized the people in their willingness to proclaim their sovereign statehood. Ironically, despite the radical, if not audacious, pronouncement of the First Amendment to the Constitution that the government of the United States of America was to be built on a secular base, the fundamental success of democracy was viewed by most citizens of the new Republic as being contingent upon an operational set of ethical-moral values and virtues. Such concepts as trust, loyalty, benevolence, unselfishness; such virtues as prudence, temperance, fortitude, and justice; and such fundamental values as faith, hope, and love were viewed as integral and basic components of democracy. What was ratified by the people of each state was more than a set of procedures for the establishment of a new government. A new way of life was ratified—indeed, a covenant was created—in which each citizen agreed to a life of service in the name of democracy. Or, in the manner of Winthrop, there was a willingness on the part of each citizen to strengthen, defend, preserve, and comfort one another; to love one another; to bear one another's burdens; to rejoice together, mourn together, labor and suffer together.

This dynamic perspective of democracy as a holistic way of life was maintained essentially intact through the first forty years of our nation's history. With the advent of Jacksonian democracy, however, fundamental changes were introduced into the system, not the least of which affected (and infected) the notions of public service, as well as the status of public administrators who bore the responsibility of maintaining the day-to-day operations of the government. This development, pejoratively described as the spoils system, is discussed in more elaborate detail in chapter 3. It is important to note at this point, however, that despite the introduction of the spoils system during the Jackson administration, and its steady virulent expansion over the next fifty years, the viable pattern of transcendent democratic values embedded in the public-service mentality at the outset of the Republic was never completely eradicated. Thus, one can say that, beginning in 1829, a second value-focused dimension—blatant, self-centered, political aggrandizement—was inviodiously added to our system of government in a manner that clearly overshadowed, but never extinguished, the optimistic vision of a public service dedicated to the attainment of the common good. Nevertheless, it is fair to conclude that the eloquent ethos of public service in the name of democracy became, by the last quarter of the nineteenth century, a fundamentally degenerate pathos of private plunder.

The spoils system created an endemic condition throughout government at all levels—federal, state, and local—that considerably weakened the values and virtues of democracy manifested in the early years of the Republic. Particularly in the post–Civil War period, the spoils system became symptomatic of a gravely ill society caught in the vortex of turbulent change. More to the point, however, in the day-to-day administrative operations of government, the spoils system was symptomatic of a debilitating feebleness that seriously impaired the executive mandate to ensure that the laws were faithfully implemented.

The Science of Efficiency

At the beginning of the Republic, the notion of executive faithfulness, inserted in the Constitution by the Framers (Article II, section 3), assumed as a given that such basic managerial principles as efficiency, effectiveness, frugality, and accountability, as well as such basic ethical values as trustworthiness, honesty, and integrity, were encompassed in the realm of faithfulness. By the last quarter of the nineteenth century, however, this assumption appeared quite dubious. Notwithstanding the sublimely benign portrait most recently advanced by Robert Maranto of the Federal Executive Institute in support of his advocacy for a return to the spoils system in the federal government,[2] many segments of society at that time were convinced that nothing short of comprehensive reform could restore public confidence in the administrative apparatus of government. One way to accomplish this end was to establish a clear-cut dichotomy between politics and administration, between policy formulation and policy implementation. A second mechanism to effect reform was the establishment of a professionalized career civil service system that would create a permanent administrative class, insulated from the perfidious currents of quadrennial political inquisitions. A third means by which integrity would, once again, be infused into the administrative system was by imposing the imprimatur of a "science of administration" on the canons of management that would henceforth prevail in the newly reformed professional environment. To ensure a clear-cut separation between policy and administration, a categorical tenet of this new "science" avowed that, with one exception, public administration should be conducted in a completely value-free context. The one exception was efficiency. Efficiency was seen as the ultimate (and only) good to be applied in gauging administrative accountability in the public sector.

The net effect of creating the twin dichotomies of politics (or policy)-administration and fact-value served to create a closed system that, buttressed by the writings of the German sociologist Max Weber and other European scholars, came to be described as the classical bureaucratic model. Dating from its fourteenth-century origins[3] and revived at the end of the nineteenth century by the writings of Weber, the concept of bureaucracy did not enjoy wide currency in the United States until the emergence of the science of administration movement. At that time, however, the grand marshals of this movement[4] essentially served notice on any who would listen that, although the values and virtues of democracy were undoubtedly worthy of pursuit, they should be pursued only by duly elected officials who were directly accountable to their respective citizen constituencies. The network that formed the career bureaucracy, on the other hand, was to be detached totally from the "hurry and strife" of a dynamic democracy. Democracy and bureaucracy did not form a seamless garment. Whatever ethical-moral impulses might invade the body politic and extend into the policymaking arenas of our governmental systems, they were to be excluded totally from the policy implementing elements of these systems.

Although the artificiality of both the policy-administration and fact-value dichotomies was evident from the outset by many insightful practitioners, in the academic community and at the more elevated levels of the administrative structure these dichotomies became, in effect, dogmas. These categorical tenets prevailed for the next fifty years, from the 1880s to the early 1930s. To maintain this illusion, especially when conflicts and contradictions inevitably arose between the values of democracy and the canons of management, a veil of hypocrisy, as discussed in chapter 2, was draped over the fault lines that separated the two systems.

In assessing the scientific management approach to public administration, two points need to be stressed. In the first place, the initial value impulse evidenced at the start of the Republic, although considerably diminished by the "spoils" mentality, was rendered even weaker by the advent of the scientific management movement. In its "scientific" environment, which stressed rational objectivity, detached impersonality, and political neutrality, there was little tolerance for the expression of the ethical-moral values and virtues associated with the common good. This original perspective was not erased from the consciousness of many public servants, but, as a result of the distinctly different values inherent in the spoils and scientific movements, it was effectively muted.

The second point that needs to be stressed in connection with the scientific management dimension is that, although the notion of a value-free administrative system was taken as a categorical imperative, the basic tenets of the movement were anything but value neutral. As previously noted, efficiency was acknowledged as the absolute good, but also included among the other "goods" to be attained were such value-loaded concepts as frugality, loyalty, obedience, subservience, impersonality, and certitude. It was this set of values that was used to shape the predominate features of public-sector management from the mid-1880s through the first third of the twentieth century, and it was no accident that these values coincided directly with the management ethos of the corporate world that emerged as a dominant force in America during this same period.

In 1887 Woodrow Wilson equated the field of public administration to that of private business.[5] Thirty-six years later, President Warren Harding, in introducing Charles Dawes, the first director of the newly created Bureau of the Budget, to his cabinet and other ranking executive officers of his administration, noted:

> This gathering has been summoned in pursuance of a policy of calling together the business heads of the government, precisely as would be done from time to time in any business organization. Here the President of the business establishment can meet those who are in direct charge of the business machinery.[6]

Dawes, in his remarks that followed, reiterated the business theme sounded by Harding and clearly defined the role of the Bureau of the Budget in classic, if somewhat embellished, terms:

> I must regard the President of the United States . . . as the head of a routine business organization, and the members of the cabinet as nothing but the administrative vice-presidents of this organization.
> . . . we [in the Budget bureau] have nothing to do with policy. Much as we love the President, if Congress, in its omnipotence over appropriations and in accordance with its authority over policy, passed a law that garbage should be put on the White House steps, it would be our regrettable duty as a bureau, in an impartial, nonpolitical, and nonpartisan way, to advise the Executive and Congress as to how the largest amount of garbage could be spread in the most expeditious and economical manner.[7]

During this period, and especially during the 1920s, the values inherent in Adam Smith's laissez-faire economics, along with the methods of management drawn from the private sector, became the driving forces of public administration. Efficiency yielded social happiness; equality was attained by allowing citizens the freedom to pursue their own goals in life, without government assistance; justice was guaranteed by the contract clause in the U.S. Constitution; and the Protestant ethic provided a moral base befitting all citizens of our society.

The fate of this rising star was determined, of course, in 1929, when the stock market crashed. The captains of industry and government maintained a stoic demeanor, but it became readily apparent that the mechanistic tenets of scientific management were ill equipped to deal with a crisis of such major proportions. A different policy perspective and a totally refitted administrative system were desperately needed. Franklin D. Roosevelt provided both in an ingenious manner by combining the humanistic values of Jefferson, the pluralistic visions of Madison, and the dynamic elements of an energetic executive embodied by Hamilton. Roosevelt and his cohorts fashioned a dynamic, proactive executive apparatus that became virtually all encompassing in its mission—to pull the nation out of the ruts of the severe economic and psychological depression. In this regard, Roosevelt revived and emphatically stressed the first value dimension of public service that was created in the initial decades of the new Republic—a democracy committed to the common good. The transcendent democratic virtues of benevolence, justice, kindness, and unselfishness became the clarion cries of the New Deal, and the foundational virtues of democracy—faith, hope, and love—became the cutting edge, so to speak, of the nation's conscience.

As discussed in chapter 5, the focus of the New Deal on the common good during the depression years yielded a fundamentally reconfigured system of democratic governance. The sharply drawn demarcation lines that had separated the bureaucratic apparatus of government from the policymaking levels were erased virtually overnight. Policy and administration became fused to the extent that relatively insignificant civil servants assumed significant roles in the shaping of public policy. Similarly, the guiding principle that came to motivate the entire executive branch was program effectiveness, rather than bureaucratic efficiency. Moreover, the concept of effectiveness was gauged primarily in qualitative terms, rather than in the exclusively quantitative measures of cost.

Throughout the Great Depression years of the 1930s and the World War II years of the 1940s, the federal executive branch became the manager of the nation. In the process, the narrow, mechanistic canons of management applied previously to gauge administrative accountability and responsibility were subordinated to the strategies and tactics that public administrators were expected to pursue in shaping political consensus. In this context, public administrators came to be viewed as major participants in the public policy process. From 1933 to 1960, another value dimension of public service, which I refer to as the pluralist-bargaining-incremental (PBI) process, took shape and became the controlling feature of our democratic political system. Essentially, the PBI process can be defined as the negotiated agreements arrived at by professional political participants over the incremental allocation of limited policy resources.

Muddling Through

Given the complexity of the nation's diversity, interest groups have always assumed a major role in the formulation of public policy. During the three decades from 1930 through the 1950s, a four-cornered "game" prevailed among interest-group representatives (lobbyists and their staffs), top-level executive officials, career administrative personnel, and congressional committees and subcommittees (and their staffs). Collectively, this set of individuals constituted a closed network of professional political participants. The demands for government resources emanating from the multitude of diverse groups in the body politic invariably exceeded the supply of resources available for allocation. Since it was assumed that these four subsets of individuals, acting in concert, would reflect the interests of their respective constituencies with a relatively high degree of accuracy, the shaping of political consensus among these subsets became the ultimate end of the PBI process.

Ideally, the optimum result of the PBI approach was to achieve a "no-lose" situation for those segments of society represented in the allocation process. As Charles Lindblom, the leading PBI advocate at the time, observed: "the policies that survive are typically presented as benefitting everybody, or everybody in a certain group, without affecting anyone outside it adversely."[8] Thus, the essence of achieving agreement in the PBI process was through mutual accommodation and compromise among the four sets of professional political participants. For groups or individuals who were allocated less than they thought they deserved, or who were passed over in the distribution process, Lindblom offered the hope of tomorrow: "any given state of affairs or combination of policies is viewed as only temporary.... As long as the policy making situation is fluid ... there will always be a tomorrow where inequities can be righted."[9] Viewed in retrospect, it is apparent that Lindblom's comment revealed the greatest strength of the PBI process in theory, and its greatest weakness in practice, for two reasons.

In the first place, it proved extremely difficult to effect any new, major resource allocations to those segments of society that did not have a viable voice in the closed, inner circle of the PBI system. The "professionals" were the full-time political actors who were masters of the intricacies of the political and bargaining processes. When those who shared the common rules of the game were in control of the policy process, stability, order, and agreement were most likely to prevail. For the process to work effectively, the most important requirement was that the bargaining arena remain closed to the uninitiated—that is, those who were not privy to the rules of the game. Once amateur political advocates entered into the bargaining arena and became involved in the final outcomes of a particular conflict, the professionals found their usual wide freedom of maneuverability severely restricted.

In the second place, a primary assumption of the PBI disciples was that the future was but an extension of the present, which in turn was shaped by the past. The validity of this assumption depended on two conditions being met. One was the maintenance of a stable external environment where both the frequency and intensity of demands for change were of such low levels that they could be accommodated by a purely reactive response sufficient to negate or dissolve the discordant situation. In this connection, it is important to note that, of the four sets of professionals involved in shaping policy outputs, the primary burden for devising appropriate reactive responses to nonprogrammed, nonroutinized demands for change fell on the career program administrators. The second condition that had to be met in order to validate the past as an accurate predictor of the future was an expanding economy. The PBI vision was centrally focused on the continued growth of the resource pie. To reduce the size of the pie was to disrupt the stability of the system and to trigger the intensity and frequency of demands for change. As long as these two conditions could be met, the PBI process was secure in its confidence that the future was simply an extension of the present, which was shaped by the past.

Unfortunately, by the beginning of the Kennedy administration in 1961, the international and domestic policy environments of the government were becoming progressively destabilized. The policies of the Eisenhower administration to contain the communist threat in Southeast Asia and to defuse the doomsday scenario of the domino theory were inherited by Kennedy. Domestically, the 1954 decision of the U.S. Supreme Court that declared racial segregation in the public schools unconstitutional marked the beginning of a new era in American democracy. Less dramatically, perhaps, but still of considerable significance, it revealed another fundamental flaw in the PBI schema.

Given the nature of public policy conflict, the notions of winning and losing, or gains and losses, are basic concerns. The key to the successful implementation of the PBI strategy was to avoid zero-sum situations. In devising the allocation formulas for any particular fiscal year, every effort was made to ensure that all groups effectively represented in the PBI arena received, at least, a thin slice of the pie. On occasion, however, some groups had to be called upon to absorb incremental losses, with the tacit understanding that such losses would be offset by subsequent gains. In other words, the integrity of the PBI process rested on the basic presumption that losses would not become cumulative for any single influential group in society. In the event that inequities were not corrected—that is, if losses did become cumulative to the point where they could never be offset by future *incremental* gains—the rationale for continuing to observe the rules of the game was totally undercut. Thus, the 1954 decision by the Supreme Court to end the separate-but-equal doctrine that had prevailed throughout the nation since 1896 did more than end segregation in the public schools. It marked the beginning of a steady (and often tumultuous) effort on the part of black Americans to demonstrate dramatically that the losses they had incurred over the years could never be offset solely by the token allocation of *incremental* gains.

As a result of these dynamic developments in both the international and domestic environments, it became increasingly apparent that the PBI system could not sustain a condition of dynamic turbulence. When the forces of change reached extreme proportions during the 1960s and 1970s, the programmed, routinized, and purely reactive responses of the career public service were incapable of achieving political consensus. A new framework for policy formulation had to be charted; a new administrative perspective had to be devised; and, in the process of doing so, a theme from the past that had been dormant for some thirty years—scientific management—was reincarnated in a more elaborate and formal mode known as rational-comprehensive analysis, also referred to initially as planning-programming-budgeting systems.

A New Perspective

Years ago, the American philosopher Walter Kaufmann, in the introduction to his reader entitled *Existentialism from Dostoevsky to Sartre*, wrote that "existentialism without Nietzsche would be almost like Thomism without Aristotle; but to call Nietzsche an existentialist is a little like calling Aristotle a Thomist."[10] Much the same can be said of the relationship between rational comprehensive analysis and the earlier mindset of scientific management; you cannot fully appreciate the former without a basic understanding of the latter, but to equate the two is like comparing apples to oranges, or, as Kaufmann said, like calling Aristotle a Thomist.

In the earlier scientific management mode of thinking, the executive branch of government was viewed as a mechanical system in which the whole was equal to the sum of its parts. This view applied to each department, to every bureau in each department, and, indeed, to every office in each bureau. This model obviously reflected the basic tenets of Max Weber's classical bureaucratic model, in which "the individual bureaucrat cannot squirm out of the apparatus in which he is harnessed ... [he] is chained to his activity by his entire material and ideal existence ... he is only a cog in an ever-moving mechanism which prescribes to him an essentially fixed route of march."[11] Moreover, as noted previously, the primary, if not exclusive, objective of this mechanistic structure was efficiency, and efficiency was defined *solely* in terms of cost reduction—the lower the cost, the greater the efficiency.

The scientific management approach was based on objective, rational (i.e., value-free) calculations and it certainly was comprehensive in its scope; every individual public administrator was expected to function as a "cog" in the most frugal manner feasible. Despite the quasi rational-comprehensive nature of the scientific management approach, it had little else in common with the rational-comprehensive design of planning-programming-budgeting systems (PPBS or, simply, PPB) introduced into the Defense Department (DOD) in 1961 by President John F. Kennedy's newly appointed secretary of defense, Robert McNamara.

The basic theoretical underpinning of PPB was systems theory, which was fundamentally different from the simple mechanistic theory that energized the earlier scientific management movement. A system is any set of components linked together to achieve a common end. Moreover, every component, which also can be termed a subsystem, is, in itself, a system, consisting of its own distinct set of components, or subsystems. Every system is purposeful and, since every system is also considered a subsystem in a higher-order system, the goal or end of one system is viewed simply as a means to the end of a higher-order system.

The prevailing view of the scientific management proponents was that the mechanical systems that governed public-sector bureaucracy were essentially static in nature and purely introspective in scope. That is to say, attention was focused exclusively on inputs, not outputs. By contrast, the basic premise of the rational-comprehensive systems theorists who devised PPB for the Defense Department was that every organizational component in the DOD operated in dynamically charged internal and external environments that were subject to constant change. Therefore, if the DOD was to perform its purposeful mission effectively, every subsystem in the department had to adapt to the forces of change in its internal and external environments. In addition, every subsystem in the department was held accountable for a measure of performance focused on outputs, not inputs.

The overall mission of the DOD was redefined in terms of broad, overarching programmatic foci, and the subsystems in the department were realigned in a crosscutting fashion that created clusters of subunits whose purposeful objectives related to one of the macro missions of the department. It then became incumbent upon *all* subunits, starting at the lowest level feasible, to define their own specific missions in a manner consistent with one of the department's overall missions and to stipulate explicitly how their missions would be changed over a projected five-year period to enhance the overall effectiveness of the department. This constituted the planning aspect of the PPB approach.

The next step required of each subunit was to devise from its planned projections a set of specific programs designed to achieve the stated objectives. In turn, each program was to be presented in terms of alternative scenarios (e.g., most favorable outcome, satisfactory outcome, least favorable outcome); the costs and benefits of each alternative scenario were to be calculated; and cost-benefit ratios were to be assigned to each. Objective, factual data obviously were to be utilized in calculating costs and benefits, but subjective, value-based *assumptions* could also be utilized as long as these assumptions were made explicit. The final step in the PPB process was to transpose the proposed programs into a specific budgetary format.

Each unit's PPB "document" would then be moved forward to be reviewed at the next higher level. The document could be returned to the subunit for revision, but when finally accepted, it became integrated in a systemwide document, which in turn was forwarded to the next system level, where the review process would be repeated, and so forth, until a totally integrated departmental document was formally adopted.

Obviously, the mindset required of the policy analysts and program managers who were to assume major roles in the PPB process was fundamentally different from that which shaped the thinking of conventional bureaucrats schooled in the weblike patterns of the PBI process. The advantages to be gained from PPB were clarity, comprehension, comprehensiveness, increased adaptability to change, and increased accountability. By far, however, the greatest advantage to be derived was an end to the internecine political warfare that was shamelessly conducted in the inner sanctums of the PBI arena by the separate branches of the military. Once PPB was firmly established, the Defense Department, for the first time since its creation, was capable of being presented by its secretary as a single, integrated system.

PPB had several factors in its favor, starting off as it did in the Defense Department. Secretary McNamara not only was the leading advocate of PPB; he understood the then-arcane science of systems theory thoroughly. Moreover, he brought with him to the Defense Department an extremely able group of young acolytes who came to be referred to as McNamara's "whiz kids." These individuals served as the vanguard in educating the DOD, Congress, and the general public on the intricacies of strategic planning, policy analysis, and performance measurement. Moreover, the DOD was the ideal agency for this new initiative. It was a hardware intensive and logistically driven operation that lent itself perfectly to quantitative analysis and measurement. So impressed was President Lyndon Johnson with McNamara's transformation of the DOD that he decreed, in a 1965 Executive Order, that PPB be adopted by all agencies in the federal government. Interestingly, in his Executive Order announcement, Johnson sounded a theme that certainly would have brought nods of approval from the ghosts of Warren Harding and Charles Dawes: "The objective of this program is simple: to use the most modern management tools so that the full promise of a finer life can be brought to every American at the least possible cost."[12]

Costs, Benefits, and Performance

On the basis of hindsight, one can say that the introduction of PPB to the Defense Department in 1961 was a watershed event in the history of public-sector management in the United States. To be sure, its life span was, as Thomas Hobbes, a seventeenth-century English political theorist, would say: "solitary, poor, nasty, brutish, and [measured in real time] short." PPB was rescinded shortly after Richard Nixon became president. The habits established by PPB, however, took deep root, not only at the federal level but also at numerous state and local jurisdictions in which it was adopted. The reason is fairly straightforward: Any public-sector agency that can (1) devise a unified, comprehensive representation of its strategic, long-range plans depicting how the agency intends to enhance the well-being of its mandated constituency and (2) can provide firm and valid performance measures that demonstrate increasingly favorable benefit-cost ratios will normally find itself in an advantageous position vis-à-vis its legislative authorization and appropriations committees.

For this reason, although PPB, per se, was formally rescinded, the basic premises on which rational-comprehensive analysis was designed persisted to reappear in one guise or another. At the federal level, PPB was followed during the Nixon years with management-by-objectives. This approach gave way, during the Carter administration, to zero-based budgeting. Although ZBB was rescinded in 1981, some elements of this management design continued in effect long after ZBB was put to rest. Most notably, the requirement for agencies to identify their key decision units and to prepare consolidated rankings remained in effect until 1986. In addition, requirements to identify three funding levels and a consolidated ranking of program elements to these funding levels were maintained until 1994.

During this period (1961–present), the advantages gained by federal executive agencies in linking the strategies and tactics of rational-comprehensive planning to program performance, and in turn to funding levels, were not lost on Congress. Although it was initially unprepared to evaluate competently the authorization and appropriation proposals submitted by executive agencies in this new format, Congress applied itself diligently to close the knowledge gap. As a result of the experience gained in working with the various iterations of the new management formats, Congress in 1993 passed the landmark Government Performance and Results Act (GPRA) in a move to show its determination to hold federal agencies accountable for their performance. For the first time in the history of the nation, Congress is now statutorily empowered to require executive agencies (1) to develop comprehensive strategic plans that define their missions in specific operational terms, (2) to define explicitly the projected results expected from these operational programs, and (3) to demonstrate that the agencies' relevant set of "stakeholders" has been fully consulted in the formulation of the agencies' strategic plans and operational programs. The act also requires agencies to develop performance measures that can (1) demonstrate the rela-

15

tionship between expected and actual results, (2) identify performance gaps, and (3) reveal the need for the realignment of program
priorities. Finally, the act requires that each agency's performance
and results document be fully integrated with the agency's budget requests.

The passage of GPRA in 1993 coincided with a parallel development in the executive branch. In March 1993 President Clinton
appointed Vice-President Gore to conduct a six-month review of the
federal executive branch to determine how "to make government
work better and *cost less.*" The final product of this undertaking was
the *Report of the National Performance Review*, also referred to as
the Gore Report, submitted to the president in September 1993.
Adopting the premises of Osborne and Gaebler's book, *Reinventing
Government*, the Gore Report advanced a set of proposals designed
to streamline the bureaucracy by reengineering the existing management structures. The two main objectives of the reinvention proposals advanced in the report were a reduction of 252,000 positions in
the federal civilian workforce over a five-year period, and a total
five-year savings of $108 billion. The president, of course, adopted
the report and ordered its immediate implementation. In his 1998
State of the Union address, President Clinton announced that both
of the specific targets—reduction of the workforce and dollar savings—had been reached and that the principal objectives of the Gore
Report had been attained: government was working better and cost-
ing less.

These two efforts—the reinventing/reengineering designs of the
executive branch and the managing for results perspective of Congress—represent the present status of a process that began with PPB
in 1961. Moreover, the two efforts are, obviously, not antithetical.
The fundamental message they both transmit, however, cuts much
deeper into the core of our democratic fiber than simply getting government to work better and cost less.

Any public-sector management strategy that is principally fixed
on a benefit-cost ratio will inevitably be confronted with some very
difficult either/or choices. President Johnson confronted this dilemma in simultaneously attempting to implement his Great Society
program *and* conduct a major war in Vietnam. The basic benefit-
cost philosophy that drove PPB at that time, however, led Johnson

to conclude that he did not have to choose between "guns and butter." Instead, an incremental increase in costs would yield, as a result of the multiplier effect, proportionately greater increased benefits. Thus, the nation could have both "guns *and* butter." During the Nixon administration this perspective was considerably attenuated, although it was never totally eliminated. Indeed, one could argue that Nixon's revenue-sharing programs resulted in increased costs and decreased benefits. The advent of the Carter administration marked a vigorous reassertion of the "multiplier" assumptions that had guided the Johnson years. Under the rubric of ZBB, the policy domain of the federal government expanded dramatically, all on the assumption that an increase in costs would yield a proportionately greater increase in benefits. Needless to say, the election of Ronald Reagan brought this kind of thinking to an end, and during the Reagan-Bush years the dominant philosophy was a contemporary variant of that which had prevailed throughout the 1920s.

As mentioned previously, the basic attitude brought to public-sector management by Harding and his budget director, Charles Dawes, was that efficiency was a direct function of costs. Decreased costs, by definition, meant increased efficiency, which was the only benefit that government should attempt to maximize. Reagan, of course, faced a much more formidable challenge than Harding. Rescinding various federal programs and deregulating large components of the economy are options to reduce costs and the size of the federal bureaucracy, and these options were vigorously pursued by the Reagan administration. At a certain point, however, negative feedback began to build up from the public. Citizens wanted to get the all-pervasive Carterized presence of government out of their lives. That is to say, they wanted the costly burdens of government removed, but they did not want a substantial reduction in the benefits government provided. How could this conundrum be resolved? One option was to assert that the implementation of public policy was best achieved through the scope and methods of private-sector management.

The notion of privatization can follow two directions. It can mean the literal transfer of specific public programs to private corporations in return for increased benefits and decreased costs, contractually stipulated. It can also mean the adoption of the strategic planning processes of the private sector by the public bureaucracies. And, of course, it can mean both. The managing-for-results attitude currently reflected in Congress favors the direct transfer of programs to the private sector. The reinventing government movement that influenced the recommendations of the Gore Report is principally focused on getting public-sector managers to think and act like private-sector entrepreneurs. It is probably for this reason that the word "customer" appears in the Gore Report 214 times, while the word "citizen" appears only 18 times.

Who Needs Ethics?

Clearly, the administrative elements that are so critically important in maintaining a viable democratic government in our society have undergone radical changes during the twentieth century. But now, at the end of the century, we are faced with a new reality in which the citizen has been reinvented into the customer; interest groups— broadly defined to include private-sector contractors, suppliers, and so on—have been redesignated stakeholders; and, most significantly, public servants have been recast in the mold of entrepreneurs. In the process of reconfiguring public bureaucracies, however, little attention is being given to how this new reality conforms to the ethical-moral values and virtues that are deeply embedded in our democratic system.

For example, citizens may very well identify themselves as customers when choosing to patronize the U.S. Postal Service, given the wide range of private-sector competitors available. Consider, however, the words chiseled in one of the cornerstones of the Old Post Office Building in Washington, D.C., when it was constructed in 1899:

> Messenger of Sympathy and Love, Servant of the Parted Friend, Consoler of the Lonely, Bond of the Scattered Family, Enlarger of the Common Life

To cite the current jargon of today's reinventors, can we think of this beautifully poetic "vision statement" as befitting UPS or Federal Express? Moreover, as is revealed in the chapters that follow, our nation's history of more than two hundred years of public service has not been bereft of entrepreneurship. But does the entrepreneurial spirit being urged on the public bureaucracy today carry with it the same sense of dedication to one's neighbors in the name of democracy that was evidenced in earlier periods of our history?

Over the past five decades of this century, two generations of public-sector careerists have been schooled intensively in the fundamental premise, derived primarily from the private sector, that the methods of "good" management are separate and distinct from the ethical-moral values and virtues inherent in democracy. Ironically, this tack has proved to be distressingly successful. Indeed, the profession of public administration, as well as the faculties of professional schools, are under intensive fire to correct this imbalance. With an increasing sense of urgency, the evidence is mounting that the current cadres of public-sector careerists are, to put it charitably, immature in their comprehension of the ethical-moral democratic values that are integrally related to the notion of public service. The fundamental question that is constantly reiterated in a wide variety of forums is this: Why are individuals being prepared to enter the public service without adequate training in ethical decision making? Indeed, professional schools have become very competent in training their students as to what they *can* do, and, as a consequence, many of these young professionals are anxious to attack the twenty-first century with a vengeance. For the most part, however, they are woefully inadequate in their efforts to prepare these same students to decide what they *should* do when faced with the distorted dynamics of a work ethic whose role models are "reinvented" clones of the Machiavellian school of management. In all honesty, it seems that the extent of our ethical knowledge base, as noted many years ago by the venerable political scientist Earl Latham, "is roughly at about the stage medicine was when the cure for typhoid was a ritual dance by a man with deer horns and a rattle."[13]

To be sure, research recently conducted by Donald Menzel reveals encouraging evidence that positive steps are being taken by accredited professional programs offering the Master of Public Administration degree to expose their students to formal ethics instruction.[14] Over the past twenty-five years there has been a steady increase in the number of accredited MPA programs that have inserted ethics courses in their curriculums. According to Menzel, by the mid-1990s formal ethics courses were offered in seventy-eight programs. Moreover, the responses of the graduates of four programs (N = 266) that were selected by Menzel for in-depth analysis were strongly positive in their endorsement of ethics instruction. Ninety percent felt that an ethics course should be required of all students, 81 percent found the subject matter valuable, and 74 percent thought their courses were stimulating. If Menzel's data are studied carefully, however, there appears to be a downside to his reported results.

The seventy-eight programs that offer formal courses in ethics constitute only 35 percent of the total number of accredited programs. In addition, ethics is a required course in only twenty, or 9 percent, of all accredited programs. Moreover, of the 266 graduates who responded to the in-depth study, nearly 80 percent confirmed that they had personally faced one or more ethical dilemmas on their jobs over the past five years. Only 42 percent, however, could positively say that their ethics education helped them resolve the dilemmas they confronted (no = 30 percent, unsure = 28 percent). Perhaps the most interesting, if not the most distressing, finding advanced in Menzel's excellent study was that 20 percent of the 266 respondents confirmed that they had *not* personally faced an ethical dilemma over the past five years. Given the fact that virtually every decision carries with it normative implications, it is difficult to imagine how any individual, having been exposed to a course in public-sector ethics, could reach such a conclusion. Relatively speaking, some encouragement can be drawn from the Menzel study concerning the advance of ethical consciousness among public-sector administrators, but certainly not enough to dismiss Earl Latham's pithy comment of fifty years earlier.

If not much has changed since then, is it not reasonable to conclude that, perhaps, the wrong question is being raised? Rather than discussing how young professionals are to be taught to discern the value of ethical variables in the context of strategic planning and performance measurement, maybe we should wonder if ethical decision making should be discussed at all in the professional schools. Why even attempt to teach ethics if the gap between theory and practice is roughly comparable to the gap between the space explorer and the witch doctor? Indeed, if one is inclined to insist on the universal value of formal ethical training in professional schools, can the gap between that which I *can* do and that which I *should* do ever be closed? In other words, why bother about the "should" if, in the final analysis, what I *will* do is determined solely by the calculable strategies of what I can do?

One homey strategy for decision making that reached its zenith during the PBI period is eloquent in its simplicity: Who's glad? How glad? Who's mad? How mad? This basic precept of prudential pragmatism provides the decision maker with a well-focused awareness of the political realities of life. Even the most savvy political realist, however, would admit that the answers to this pragmatic formula cannot be taught; they can only be learned by those who are astutely aware of its all-pervasive presence and importance.

Much the same, it would seem, can be said about ethical-moral values that struggle for recognition in our society. If the future professionals who are now being trained to guide our society into the twenty-first century are to consider the ethical ramifications of their decisions, now is the time for them to develop an abiding and all-pervasive *ethical* sense of judgment in the same manner that political pragmatists have honed their intuitive sense of human self-interest. Unfortunately, the latter is much easier to develop than the former, probably because expediency is perceived as being more practical than prolonged reflection and discernment, pretense more effective than forthrightness, and self-interest more relevant than any higher-order abstraction. Thus, there are many more pragmatic professionals in our society than those who could be considered ethically mature.

If one is to develop a mature sense of ethical consciousness that can be focused on the professional domain of public service, three basic propositions have to be accepted as axiomatic. First, no public policy, program, or operation is value neutral when it is implemented. Second, every public policy, program, and operation has a discernible subjective impact (positive or negative) on the lives of other human beings (i.e., citizens). Third, the responsibility for the effects of these impacts rests with those who, by virtue of their professional authority (i.e., accredited competence), are either directly or indirectly involved in the decision-making processes that energize the action pathways from initiation to implementation. To be sure, accepting these three axiomatic propositions is frequently very difficult. The assumption that ethics cannot be discussed apart from the notion of personal responsibility is viewed by many as a very radical and unacceptable proposition. That is why the responses most frequently invoked to disavow the relationship between ethics and responsibility—variations of the common theme "Am I my brother's [and sister's] keeper?"—actually form the keystone of the pragmatic catechism of the political realists.

The Want of Wonder

"Am I my brother's [and sister's] keeper?" is not an idle, metaphysical speculation. To be sure, in various religious traditions the answer to this biblical question carries with it profound theological implications. If considered in terms of public service, however, the question's specific purpose is to focus attention on performance, not promise; on actions, not intentions; on purposeful ends, not expedient means; and on individual responsibility, not aggregate detachment.

The American author Herman Wouk was tremendously successful in transposing the Genesis story of Cain and Abel to a literary masterpiece entitled *The Caine Mutiny*, but he provided no definitive answer to this perennial biblical query. Instead, in masterful fashion, he skillfully and subtly moved the question, which is deeply buried in our very being, into the reader's conscious reality. Wouk understood the paradox involved—namely, one can learn that which cannot be taught. As a consequence, by subliminally focusing attention on the question "Am I my brother's [and sister's] keeper?" Wouk forced his readers to develop and refine their own "answers" into a mature conscious awareness of the fact that ethics and responsibility are indivisible.

In preparing our students for careers in public service, we lack the skill and subtlety of a Herman Wouk. Many of the millions who read his book or who saw the movie (*The Caine Mutiny*) or the play (*The Caine Mutiny Court-Martial*) came to the uncomfortable realization that, first and foremost, the notion of individual ethical responsibility is not absolved by hierarchical systems. No one who embarks on the U.S.S. *Caine* can avoid confronting the one eternal verity of ethics: the buck doesn't stop at the top. Or, to paraphrase the English poet John Donne: "Ask not where the buck stops; it stops with you."

The purported deathbed scene of another literary giant, Gertrude Stein, can be juxtaposed with the Cain and Abel story. As her devoted disciples gathered around her bed, one especially distraught follower is supposed to have burst out in despair: "Oh, Miss Stein, what is the answer?" to which Stein retorted, "What is the question?" The title of this introductory chapter also poses a question, "Is Anybody Listening?" Like Gertrude Stein's question, mine is more of a rhetorical challenge than a specific question in search of an answer. It is a question in search of a questioner, a listener, a hearer. Its only value is in the asking.

The eminent man of letters G.K. Chesterton noted long ago that the world will never suffer from the want of wonders but only from the want of wonder. Can we begin to wonder what it means to confront the question, "Am I my brother's [and sister's] keeper?" To pose this question inevitably leads us to wonder "is anybody listening?"—"does anybody care?" Exploring in depth the strategies and tactics of the current reinventing government movement might lead us to wonder further about ourselves as responsible human beings committed to a profession in the public service. In the process we can learn much about ourselves, and, indeed, we can begin to wonder if we have not learned more than we care to know. The kind of freedom attached to ethical maturity is not bought cheaply. Indeed, the ethical immaturity of the pragmatists is a gem of a bargain by comparison. If, however, one can begin to penetrate the well-guarded deceptions of these "common sense" realists, one can then begin to learn that which could never be taught, namely, that a commitment to public service demands an acutely positive and sensitive understanding of ethical-moral consciousness.

The choice to follow a professional pathway in the service of democracy should by no means be a casual decision. At the least, it means opting for a career of service to the public, to the citizenry, to one's neighbors. More significantly, however, it is a professional commitment to serve in a very specific, clearly defined context—that is, in a democracy complete with all the values, attitudes, and beliefs associated with that specific form of government. Along with the various "isms," democracy has been and continues to be studied and refined. Admittedly, a professional career in the service of democracy does not demand expert knowledge of American democratic political theory. Nevertheless, one should not be too quick in overlooking the indivisible linkage that exists between our nation's democratic political values and Judeo-Christian ethical values.

The primary purpose of this volume is to stress the significance of this relationship as it applies specifically to the career public servant and our bureaucratic-democratic ethos. The arguments advanced in the chapters that follow rest on the basic assumption that the ethical-moral values derived from the Judeo-Christian tradition form the essence of our democratic being. Thus, to commit oneself to the service of democracy requires, at least, a conscious and mature awareness of (1) the ethical impulses of democracy, (2) the transcendent values of democracy, and (3) the moral vision of democracy. Our current inability to deal comfortably and effectively with these subjects and the issues they raise is reflected in the crisis of our time. In many instances over the past several decades, our public-sector policy process has seemed anemic; our political system, immobilized; and our sense of ethical-moral purposefulness, fixed at a level of procedural legal incantations and pro forma political exhortations. Unless and until we can begin to restore the ethical impulses, the transcendent values, and the moral vision that inhere in democracy and in the ethos of public service, we will continue to drift in the backdraft of pragmatic expediency and narrow self-interest despite the efforts currently being exerted by the advocates of reinventing government.

The public service is an unlikely source to turn to for deliverance. Its infamous call name—the bureaucracy—is recognized globally, although seldom in any positive fashion. Yet, at least as far as our own democratic system is concerned, there is no alternative but to look to the "fourth branch" of government—the bureaucracy —to revive democracy's ethical impulses, transcendent values, and moral vision that have atrophied for the better part of the past half-century. Given the complexity of the policy process, the scope and magnitude of the bureaucracy, and the accumulated experience of public-sector careerists, a major share of the responsibility for maintaining the life and vitality of democracy as we enter the twenty-first century must be assumed by an ethically mature, morally conscious, and fully dedicated group of professional citizens who are committed to the fundamental democratic proposition that they *are* their brothers' and their sisters' keepers.

To be sure, such an assertion reflects a high degree of optimistic hopefulness, but certainly not the Pollyanna-like faith of a deluded apologist. In the chapters that follow, the art and craft of public-sector management are examined with the critical scrutiny of one who firmly embraces the belief that the essence of democracy is to be found in the willingness of each citizen to contribute to the well-being of another. This responsibility falls with particular force on the shoulders of those who choose a career in the service of democracy. In this context, every public servant is a citizen and every public servant is our society's primary agent to ensure that every citizen becomes a public servant. The ethical-moral dimensions of this responsibility are the basic focus of this volume, and the value in being aware of this mandate is not to be discounted cavalierly. At minimum, it enables one to nurture a critical ethical consciousness that can function as an early-warning alarm to protect those whom one is duty bound to serve.

In this connection, it may be appropriate to cite the former British prime minister Harold Macmillan, who related to the eminent philosopher of history Isaiah Berlin that he had once taken a course at Oxford offered by J.A. Smith, a Hegelian philosopher. As Macmillan recounted the anecdote,

> In his first lecture ... this professor spoke as follows: "All of you, gentlemen, will have different careers—some of you will be lawyers, some of you will be soldiers, some will be doctors or engineers, some will be government servants, or enter the Church, some will be landowners or politicians. Let me tell you at once that nothing I say during these lectures will be of the slightest use to you in any of the fields in which you will attempt to exercise your skills. But one thing I can promise you: if you continue with this course of lectures to the end, you will always be able to know when men are talking rot."[15]

If those who continue with this volume to its end are left as well prepared as they embark on the ethical-moral pathways that lead into
the next century, the hope and the vision of the Founding Fathers
will be affirmed.

2

The Dark Specter of Hypocrisy and Pretense

IN A 1977 lecture at the University of California–Berkeley, one of America's most eminent public administration scholars, Dwight Waldo, advanced a cogent and concise statement concerning the fundamental essences of democracy and bureaucracy. In so doing, he demonstrated the intrinsic tensions that exist at the interface of these two concepts. As viewed by Waldo, the counterpolar forces generated by the juxtaposition of these two concepts give rise to a third: hypocrisy.

> Hypocrisy enters because the "dialectic" between democracy and bureaucracy offers extraordinary opportunities for confusion and self-delusion and invites self-serving opinions. After all, both democracy and bureaucracy are multifaceted and controversial. When both are studied together, the opportunities for confusion and delusion are multiplied, given the human capacity for irrationality and ego-serving views of the world.[1]

One of the reasons for the confusion and delusion is that the engines of democracy and bureaucracy run on different tracks, leaving from different stations and heading for different destinations. Sometimes they run parallel to each other, seemingly moving as one; more frequently, their tracks either diverge or converge, depending on the forces exerted on them at any given time. When they do converge, the inevitable result is, as Waldo politely suggests, a dialectical "happening," by which I assume he means "a hell of a train wreck." Elsewhere in his writings, Waldo reflects on these inevitable "happenings" and concludes: "Why would an instrument [bureaucracy] designed to be impersonal and calculating be expected to be effective in delivering sympathy and compassion?"[2] One cynical answer that immediately suggests itself is that such expectations are the nurturing catalysts of hypocrisy and that the methods of allocating political power in our systems of governance thrive on the exploitation of hypocrisy. Such an explanation is, however, much too glib, too superficial. More fundamentally, the answer can be found in the manner in which we have twisted democracy to fit the cardinal canons of management, which in fact are embedded deeply in the fiber of bureaucratic systems. Viewed in this context, the essence of hypocrisy is evidenced at its most extreme.

Continuing in his Royer lecture, Waldo provides a brief and attenuated survey of classical liberal economists, public-choice economists, and contemporary liberals as examples of those who are in the vanguard of fostering hypocrisy in the most erudite manner. He then begins to draw his lecture to a close with his own personal confessional statement:

> I do not except myself from the charge of hypocrisy, indeed not. Again and again I have "caught myself" in entertaining, according to circumstance, two opinions that cannot be reconciled; or defending a position that, objectively considered, is clearly in my own self-interest. Over time, certainly, I have first accepted then rejected various positions or "solutions."[3]

My purpose in citing these personal comments is certainly not to hold our profession's distinguished sage accountable for thoughts and words recorded twenty years ago. Indeed, there is no reason to assume that he is still not rejecting a wide variety of positions or solutions that he previously embraced, including, perhaps, his position on hypocrisy as being the "black sheep" offspring of the union between democracy and bureaucracy. I would hope that the latter is not the case simply because it should be apparent that, as we prepare to cross the threshold of the twenty-first century, the predominant operational characteristic of the inherent fusion of democracy and bureaucracy—and that which, in turn, defines our deeply ingrained paradigm of policy and administration in a democratic society—is hypocrisy.

Admittedly, my sense of hypocrisy as it applies to the confluence of democracy and bureaucracy extends far beyond the modest transgressions revealed by Waldo in his Royer lecture. Those who have not experienced the agony of holding two irreconcilable positions at the same time must truly be viewed as suspect, as, indeed, are those who have never modified or rejected a position previously taken. Nevertheless, after more than 200 years of experience at laboring in the service of democracy, is it not fair to conclude that *we*—as a society, and certainly "we" as a profession—have become expert in using hypocrisy to hide the hypocrisy that has infested the core of our system of democratic governance? Perhaps now is the time for us, as a profession, to borrow a page from another distinguished scholar, Chris Argyris, and commit ourselves to "making the undiscussable and its undiscussability, discussable."[4]

The Rule of Law

One logical way to begin is to consider the historical roots of the term "hypocrisy" that stem from the Greek *hupokrisis* ("pretense") and *hupokrinesthai* ("to pretend"). Thus, we should not be surprised to learn that our current usage of the word "hypocrite" derives from the classical Greek *hupocrites* ("actor") and *hupokrinein* ("to play a part"). The hypocrite, then, is an actor, one who plays a part; who pretends by adopting an attitude that is at variance with his or her own convictions; who articulates one thing but, in fact, means something quite different.

Just how well we fit into these parameters of hypocrisy can be judged by the manner in which we still embrace the democratic rhetoric of Jefferson while continuing to act in a pragmatic manner befitting Madison. Moreover, we, as a society, continue to sanctify the virtue of union—unity through diversity—but, by the same token, we are forever loath to forgo the vigor of "rugged" individualism as the categorical imperative of freedom. For public administrators who must operate in this convoluted system of democratic values and who must, at the same time, recognize the intrinsic values of bureaucracy and its attendant canons of management, the art of pretense, the methods of acting or of playing a role—indeed, of wearing a mask—become virtual prerequisites for a successful career.

Interestingly, however, there is another Hellenistic imprint reflected in the terms *hupokrisis* ("pretense") and *hupocrites* ("actor"). In the days of Homer, the original verb, *krinesthai,* meant "to interpret (e.g., dreams)." In Attic Greek it was given a slight shift of meaning in the direction of "answer," and it was only in the later Greek that the interpretation became identified with an actor's performance on the stage. Thus, the original meaning of the word in the Greek world was defined in terms of reciting, interpreting, and answering.

Needless to say, to recite, to interpret, to answer are not incidental functions of public servants. In both the early Greek and Jewish traditions, there were particular individuals who served the important function of transmitting sacred knowledge from its divine source to the people. This task fell to those who had wisdom and understanding. In Greece, it was the poets who interpreted the dictates of its gods. For the Israelites, this task was assumed by the prophets, who received their instructions directly from God. In the New Testament, however, the terms "hypocrite" and "hypocrisy" were more pointedly defined to mean an ability to render fine-tuned legal distinctions, to interpret God's Law with hairsplitting scrupulosity. This connotation of hypocrisy is revealed most emphatically in the Gospel writings of Matthew. Indeed, at no other point in the entire Bible is the word "hypocrite" used with such focused vehemence as that reflected in the torrent of anger leveled by Jesus at a group of God's servants. In what is commonly referred to as the "Seven Woes" passage, the phrase "Woe unto you, scribes [i.e., lawyers] and Pharisees, hypocrites!" is repeated six times (with one other "Woe to you, blind guides" passage included), and each is followed by a stinging denunciation of the manner in which they apply the Law with absolute, minute precision.[5]

As recorded by Matthew, the manner in which the Pharisees and scribes proceeded to carry out their functions as the reciters and interpreters of God's Law with absolute scrupulosity was at wide variance with the true intent of His Law. Thus, it comes about that the notion of scrupulosity is subsequently identified by Paul Ricoeur, the French philosopher, as

a delicate consciousness, a precise consciousness enamored of increasing perfection; it is a consciousness anxious to observe all the commandments, to satisfy the law in all things, without making an exception of any sector of existence, without taking into account exterior obstacles … and which gives equal importance to little things as to great. But at the same time scrupulosity marks the entrance of moral consciousness into its own pathology; a scrupulous person encloses himself in the inextricable labyrinth of commandments; obligation takes on an enumerative and cumulative character, which contrasts with the simplicity and sobriety of the commandment to love God and man. The scrupulous consciousness never stops adding new commandments. This atomization of the law into a multitude of commandments entails an endless "juridization" of action and a quasi-obsessional ritualization of daily life. The scrupulous person never arrives at satisfying all the commandments, or even any one. At the same time even the notion of obedience is perverted; obedience to a commandment because it is commanded becomes more important than love of neighbor, or even love of God; this exactitude in observance is what we call legalism.[6]

When viewed in this context, the notion of hypocrisy suggests not only the acting out of a part through the answering of questions or the recitation and interpretation of the law, but also the indefatigable commitment to a scrupulosity that assumes all human behavior is ultimately capable of being subject to legislation.

The linkage that is forged between the notions of hypocrisy and legalism raises several basic questions that challenge us still. Indeed, most of the contemporary thinking on public-sector ethics, for example, is virtually uniform in its support of the notion that the scrupulous avoidance of the wrong is tantamount to fulfilling the right, and that the qualitative values of democratic responsibility can be satisfied by adhering to the mechanistic minutiae of procedure. Is there more to public service than the assiduous implementation of statutory directives? Is there more to justice than the scrupulous adherence to the law? Is it stretching the point too far to suggest that our contemporary public servants, who recite, interpret, and answer—that is, implement—the laws, are the direct-line descendants of the poets and prophets of a distant age? Or is it more accurate to link our public-sector managers and administrators to the mechanistic and myopic vision of the Pharisees and scribes who were so caustically denounced as hypocrites in Matthew's Gospel?

The distinguished political scientist Norton Long noted some years ago, "Law in action is administration." Does it not then follow—given the political philosophy we, as a nation, embrace—that administration in action must reflect the organic essence of democracy? Or are public servants simply mandated to follow the narrow dictum so cogently articulated more than fifty years ago by the political theorist Herman Finer who, in the classic Friedrich-Finer debate, was adamant in his insistence that "the servants of the public ... are to be responsible to the elected representatives of the public, and these [elected representatives] are to determine the course of action of the public servants to the most minute degree that is technically feasible."[7]

To be sure, the functions of democracy inhere in the rule of law, and we constantly reaffirm the honored shibboleth, advanced by John Adams in drafting the original Massachusetts constitution, that ours is "a government of laws and not of men." But as former U.S. Supreme Court Justice Jerome Frank once wrote:

Hypnotized by those words, we picture as an existing reality—or at least as a completely achievable ideal—a government so contrived that it matters not at all what men, at any given moment, constitute government. Such an idea is a narcotic. It is bad medicine. It does not protect us from bad government. On the contrary, it invites bad government.

Additionally, Frank noted:

It is imperative that in a democracy it should never be forgotten that public office is, of necessity, held by mere men with human frailties. To *pretend*, then, that government, in any of its phases, is a machine—that it is not a human affair; that the language of statutes—if only they were adequately worded—plus appeals to the upper courts, will alone do away with the effect of human weaknesses in government officials is to worship illusion. And it is a dangerous illusion.[8]

The functions of democracy may very well be intrinsic to the rule of law, but the manner in which the laws are administered—whether by modern-day poets and prophets or by the contemporary counterparts to the Pharisees and scribes—will determine if the faith we invest in our reverence for the law is well founded or simply a dangerous illusion. While public administrators must be solidly grounded in the reason and reverence of the law, they should also be alert to another reality advanced by the eminent Protestant theologian Reinhold Niebuhr: "it must be observed that reason may provide the law but not, of itself, furnish the reverence."[9] Niebuhr's point is similar to his comment on justice: "Any justice which is only justice soon degenerates into something less than justice. It must be saved by something which is more than justice."[10] But what is the "more than"?

Given Niebuhr's primary focus, the answer obviously moves in a theological direction. A more secular, but nonetheless holistic, answer can be derived from an early twentieth-century management scholar and consultant, Mary Parker Follett. In the following excerpt from her book *Creative Experience*, Follett refers specifically to our judicial system. If her basic terms of reference, however, are replaced with those enclosed in brackets, the relevant insights of her comments remain undiminished.

> Perhaps the most widespread fallacy in regard to law is that its chief aim is the preservation of peace and order. The administration of justice is not the orderly disposition of controversies; the administration of justice must be truly part of that social process which generates ever those further activities which are significant for the progress of men.... Not "law and order," but to make conflict creative must be the part of law as of every other activity of our life.... The legal [administrative] order by helping to integrate purposes is helping to produce larger purposes. The judicial [administrative] decision must anticipate this process. It must

meet the larger purpose even though the larger purpose does not exist until the contribution of that very decision has been made. Thus, the difference between declared and *de facto* purpose is more subtle than is always seen: the judge [administrator] is working for an end which does not exist as an end until he begins working for it.[11]

Viewed in the context of these comments, the role of public administration in our democratic society can hardly be overstated. The implementation of public policy—like the rule of law, or the administration of justice, or the recognition of any of the inalienable rights we revere—involves much more than the mechanistic application of statutory and programmatic directives that can be shaped solely on the basis of immediate benefit or pragmatic expediency. The administrative implementation of policy must incorporate a teleological sense of purpose that clearly transcends the exigencies of the present. To do otherwise is simply to pursue a very dangerous illusion based on pretense—that is to say, to speak the lines, to play the role, to don the mask of hypocrisy. Unfortunately, in so many elaborate ways that punctuate the public service today, the notion of hypocrisy seems destined to enter the twenty-first century carrying the same overtones of dissemblance and scrupulosity that were recognized by the ancient past.

A System of Belief

Nearly a half-century ago, one of our most eminent American historians, Perry Miller, placed the Puritan experiment under his scholarly microscope and produced a volume, modest in size but robust in substance, entitled *Errand into the Wilderness*.[12] As he explained in his opening chapter, the end result of the Puritan *experience* was significant in the shaping and building of America. On the other hand, the Puritan *experiment* to establish a theocracy in dogmatic terms, under the self-ordained, divine-like guidance of John Winthrop and others, failed abysmally. The *experiment* failed because, to cite the words of a thirteenth-century theologian, Peter Abelhard, "it is one thing ... to propagate a religion in dogmatic terms; it is another thing to ask men to look into themselves and to find there, and in the history of mankind, the data of a system of belief."[13] Thus, it was the *experience* of the undertaking that caused the early settlers, throughout all the colonies—as Abelhard anticipated and Miller confirmed—to look into themselves and into the history of mankind, in order to find the basis of a *system of belief.*

The fifty-five men who came together in Philadelphia to fashion a political document obviously had an entirely different agenda than the synod of Puritan clergy and lay elders who assembled in Boston in 1679. Under the guidance of Increase Mather, a leading Puritan theologian and future president of Harvard College, that synod met to condemn the vast moral quagmire of sins, crimes, and misdemeanors into which their followers had become immersed.[14] By contrast, there emerged from the gathering in Philadelphia a guarded, but nonetheless clearly defined, optimistic hope for the future. This sense of hope was linked to a unified sense of purpose to define the promise of a democratic polity. Thus, a system of belief emerged that was built around the notions of *individual freedom,* balanced by a clearly articulated notion of self-responsibility; *equality*—albeit narrowly drawn—balanced by a deeply felt sense of humility and unselfishness; and *justice,* balanced by a combination of sternness and benevolence. Added to these basic values that form the bedrock of democracy were the age-old cardinal virtues of prudence, temperance, fortitude, and justice, as well as the foundational virtues of the Judeo-Christian ethic—faith, hope, and love. Drawn together, these values and virtues created a centripetal nexus capable of shaping the embryo of a unique form of democracy designed to guide the new America to the common good inherent in "the good society."

From the beginning of this "errand into the wilderness," the notion of individual freedom, and its concomitant subthemes of individualism and individual self-interest, ranked paramount. The Puritans' efforts to build a theocracy in the New World, governed by dogmatic religious dictates, were an exercise in futility. Nevertheless, the 150 years or so that preceded the establishment of our present Constitution must be recognized as the gestation period for a unique form of democracy that, first and foremost, placed the notion of sovereign power in the minds and hearts of each individual citizen. This basic theorem of governance, however, was linked to an indivisible corollary, namely, a sense of unity whereby the whole was seen as greater than the sum of its parts. Thus, from the beginnings of our colonial experience, the notion that a democratically governed system of human endeavor could be designed to achieve a common sense of unity became the ultimate purposeful end of American democracy. The nation's basic, organic documents cannot be understood if read as dogmatically defined legal tracts. As Alexis de Tocqueville, the French statesman and historian, so astutely observed:

> The government of the Union depends almost entirely upon legal *fictions;* the Union is an *ideal nation* which exists ... *only in the mind,* and whose limit and extent can *only* be discerned by the understanding.... The Constitution of the United States resembles those *fine creations* of human industry which ensure wealth and renown to their inventors, but which are profitless in other hands.[15]

The documents themselves reflected the intentions of the Founding Fathers, and their intentions, in turn, were clearly derived from a system of belief based on the assumption that excellence in human character was certain to be reflected in the excellence of national character. "We now have a National character," George Washington wrote as the Revolutionary War was near its end, "and it is of the utmost importance to stamp favorable impressions upon it."[16] That is to say, the character of democracy is derived solely from the body, mind, and spirit of individual commitment to a common good. The Constitution and the Bill of Rights are action documents, preceded by the intentions of the Founding Fathers as stated in the Declaration of Independence and the Constitution's brief Preamble. Moreover, compacted in the Preamble are the values and virtues of a people who are infused with an eschatological vision of "the good society." Indeed, according to one of the leading scholars on the history of religion in America, Sydney Ahlstrom, at the height of the Revolutionary period,

> A new conception of freedom and equality took shape, involving conceptions of God, man, human rights, the state, and history, which became inseparable from the Enlightenment's outlook on

reality. On 4 July 1776, these conceptions became a cornerstone of the American political tradition; during this period they were given further embodiment in state constitutions (and in due course in the federal Constitution). In the words of the nation's Patriot heroes and Founding Fathers, these ideas were woven into the very texture of American thinking.[17]

Nor were the temper and tone of the new political vision overlooked by Tocqueville in 1835:

> Religion in America takes no direct part in the government of society, but nevertheless it must be regarded as the foremost of the political institutions of that country; ... I do not know whether all Americans have a sincere faith in their religion.... But I am certain that they hold it to be indispensable to the maintenance of republican institutions.[18]

Eighty years before Tocqueville, in 1755, John Adams reflected on the role of moral values in a republican democracy and concluded that

> it brings the great principle of the Law of Nature and Nations —Love your neighbor as yourself, and do to others as you would that others should do to you—to the knowledge, belief, and veneration of the whole people.... The duties and rights of the man and the citizen are thus taught from early infancy to every creature.[19]

Extending this retrospective of history even further, nearly seventy-five years before Adams wrote that comment, William Penn, the founder and long-time proprietor of Britain's most successful colony, expressed similar views in 1682 that strike a relevant chord for public administration today.

> Government itself ... [is] as capable of kindness, goodness, and charity as a more private society. They weakly err that think there is no other use of government than correction which is the coarsest part of it. Daily experience tells us that the care and regula-

tion of many other affairs, more soft and daily necessary, make up much of the greatest part of government.[20]

Undoubtedly, among the fifty-five men who gathered in Philadelphia to draft the Constitution, as well as among the citizens of the thirteen states who awaited the outcome of the Framers' deliberations, there existed a high degree of anxiety concerning the practical and pragmatic obstacles that threatened the fragile state of independence gained in 1776. Fortunately, the Framers were able to draw on an extensive body of experience to serve as their guide. Unlike the Puritans who founded the Massachusetts Bay colony with a utopian vision, the Framers used as their practical benchmark the *system of belief* that had evolved in the colonies over the previous 150 years. The ideas that constituted this system of belief included their conceptions of the values and virtues associated with the spirit of democracy. These ideas reflected their notions of God, human dignity, individual freedom, communal responsibility, and justice. It was *their* practical, pragmatic nature, however, that gave their "experiment" greater hope for success than the Puritans' undertaking. The Framers made no effort to fashion a seamless garment, good for all time, but only one that was serviceable and adaptable to change. Nevertheless, woven throughout the garment were the ethical values and moral virtues that formed the core of their system of belief. These constituted an indivisible presence in all of the practical and pragmatic decisions made concerning the structure and functions of the new government.

The Irony of Unreality

In the grand span of civilization, 200 years are a raindrop in the ocean of time. Nevertheless, since the founding of our Republic, a discomforting irony can be clearly discerned in connection with the ethical values and moral virtues generally assumed to infuse American democratic theory. That is to say, when our new nation stepped into the nineteenth century, the neophytes who constituted the government depended heavily on a relatively firm consensual base of civic morality and its attendant ethical values in building a system of governance, including the formulation of its laws. At the present time, however, as we prepare to enter the twenty-first century, the nation—over 200 years older and ostensibly wiser—is almost totally reliant on its laws and its lawmakers to define the ethical-moral values and virtues that inhere in democracy. One immediate consequence of this charade is that it represents a crowning triumph of democratic hypocrisy. A second and more directly relevant consequence is that it places public administrators at all levels of government in the untenable position of having to apply processes that are devoid of any purposeful vision other than the immediate realization of narrow, particularistic self-interests.

Two hundred years ago, this was not the case. Drawing from a common source, that is, the history of Western civilization—and, particularly from that history, the progressive evolution of democratic governance—the Founding Fathers, in shaping the foundational documents of the new Republic, gave hardly any explicit attention to the notion of administration. Obviously, in their minds, as in Waldo's, the linkages between civilization and administration were conterminous and formed a cohesive system of belief.

"There is an intricate and intimate relationship between civilization and administration," Dwight Waldo stated in one of the valedictory lectures given during his final semester at the Maxwell School in 1979. "Administration was present 'at the Creation,'" he tells us. "It was an integral part of civilization whenever and wherever civilization developed; and without the foundation and framework it supplied, civilization would not have developed."[21]

Waldo's point is, as he claims in that lecture, clearly unassailable. In every human sociopolitical grouping, in whatever manner classified by history, the basic functions associated with the acquisition and allocation of resources (however defined), the maintenance of an internal sense of orderliness, and the collective mobilization for the common defense against external threats have been evidenced. Beginning with its most rudimentary forms, the history of civilization has been a progression of increased administrative complexity and sophistication. To appreciate fully this symbiotic relationship, and particularly its relationship to the advent of democracy in America, some more detail needs to be inserted.

Obviously, administrative actions do not occur in a vacuum.

Viewed in macro terms, the history of administration is a history of service to some higher authority. As such, it is a history of willing subordination, loyalty, obedience, courage, and expertise. Given the best of all rational worlds, human intentions precede action, which is to say, purpose precedes process and policy directs administration. To be sure, at the micro levels, the history of administration is replete with examples of what we commonly refer to as administrative discretion. In all such instances, however, history consistently confirms that one cardinal rule prevails, namely, any such discretionary acts by subordinates can be legitimized only to the extent that they are faithfully congruent to the intended purposes of the superior authority.

Having said this, it should be apparent that this amazingly consistent historical pattern of administrative structures, functions, processes, procedures, and behavior can be, and has been, utilized to serve virtually *any* purposeful end as determined by the relevant higher authority. Thus, when the phenomenon we call bureaucracy is linked to a specific form of governance we call democracy, we must assume—given even the most basic understanding of rational behavior—that the former will act in a manner congruent to and consistent with the intentions of the latter. In this regard, therefore, it certainly is reasonable to ask, what purpose does democracy serve? That is to say, what is its purposeful goal? Among the many and various forms of governance recorded in the annals of modern civilization alone, democracy is widely extolled as the universal *good*. But what is it good for? These questions are not advanced as idle abstractions; the manner in which they are answered should define the intentional impulses that trigger administrative actions in a democratic society.

To view the history of administration in terms of service to some higher authority is to suggest that the notion of duty is a principal characteristic of such a commitment. As I have suggested here and elsewhere,[22] many of the key figures who were present at the creation of our Republic were implicitly bound to a transcendent sense of duty that was teleologically fixed to the future. This sense of duty was, in turn, imparted to the administrative mainstream in the form of a public-service imperative that would validate the actions of those who obeyed it.

The notion of duty as a categorical imperative related to public service is fairly straightforward. Public servants are those who obey the directives of "higher authority" with loyal and trusting responses, which is to say, "no questions asked." Nevertheless, if this notion of duty is considered in terms of the manner in which bureaucracy should be related to democracy, one is confronted with a dilemma of major proportions.

If service is defined solely in terms of duty, the values of obedience, loyalty, trust, and courage can, indeed, be indelibly imprinted on the cardinal virtues of prudence, fortitude, temperance, and justice, but the net result in far too many historical circumstances has been the manifestation of pretense. That is to say, far too often the *appearance* of a commitment to duty is sufficient to fulfill the demands of service, and as a consequence the individual who is successful in *appearing* to be a dutiful public servant is most frequently viewed as an exemplary bureaucrat.

The effort to create a pretension of service by maintaining a convincing appearance of duty characterizes the type of artificial administrator that is, by no means, an anomaly in public-sector organizations. Perhaps, in this regard, it would be well to recall the indomitable cynicism of Oscar Wilde, the Irish poet, playwright, and wit: "The first duty of life is to be as artificial as possible. What the second duty is no one has yet discovered."[23] Unfortunately, far too many of even the most competent and dedicated career civil servants, at some point in their professional careers, have become seduced by the pretense of duty. They appear, to utilize the words of the biblical prophet Jeremiah, "like scarecrows in a cucumber field and they cannot speak; they have to be carried for they cannot walk. Be not afraid of them, for they cannot do evil; neither is it in them to do good."[24]

Moreover, in attempting to maintain the artificial appearance of duty, many public administrators have sought to link their commitment of service to the amoral pretense of detached objectivity, neutral competence, and dispassionate rationality. Admittedly, the rationale that undergirds this perspective has a long and impressive legacy in the history of administration. In theory, this concept also appears unassailable, especially when related to a system of democratic governance. As a means to a higher end, the notion of administrative neutrality rests on the assumption that administrative subordinates, working behind the screen of anonymity, will provide the elected representatives of the people with a steady flow of objective, accurate, and pertinent information. From this primary source, the representatives will then be able to arrive at sound, rational, and defensible policy decisions that accord with the public interest. In point of fact, however, history informs us that seldom is the true purity of this means-end relationship realized.

In far too many instances—and, particularly, in these last decades of the twentieth century—the notion of administrative neutrality has routinely devolved into an end in itself, thus falling victim to the irony of unreality. As Viktor Frankl, the Viennese psychiatrist, once noted, "The capacity of seeing is dependent on the incapacity of the eye to see itself."[25] Does it not follow, therefore, that once public administrators become self-consciously "neutral," their roles in the democratic process become effectively "neutered" and, hence, rendered essentially dysfunctional? One could persuasively argue that, beginning in the early 1950s, the notion of administrative neutrality devolved into a programmed—that is, habituated—response[26] that, in fact, contaminated the democratic process by transfusing a bitter unreality into the lifeblood of the common good. If one adds scrupulosity to the element of a self-conscious neutrality, all the conditions necessary for a full-blown state of hypocrisy are present.

There is, however, a more fundamental question that can be raised concerning the efficacy of objective neutrality and its counterpart, subjective detachment. Viewed from a reductionist perspective, any complex policy proposal or problem situation can be reduced to a series of segmented parts. In this context, each part of the whole can be dealt with independently, with detached objectivity, by distinct teams of administrative specialists. Nobel Laureate Herbert Simon's "watchmaker"—that is, the relevant higher authority—will then be responsible for assembling the parts into a finished product —that is, a policy proposal or a problem solution.[27] In this mechanistic framework, individual administrative specialists need concern themselves only with the part-of-the-whole assigned to their respective groups. The basic question each discrete team is required to answer is "what can I do?" in this segmented aspect of the policy/problem situation. The more fundamental question—"What should I do?"—is not the responsibility of *any* of the segmented teams, but only of the "watchmaker." In this context, the notions of neutrality, disinterestedness, and detachment can flow as smoothly as a duck lands on water.

A contrary view, however, can be argued more persuasively. If public administrators see themselves as operating in a holistic system of democratic values, virtues, and vision—and, furthermore, if they see themselves as assuming an integral role in contributing to the ultimate purposefulness of democracy—is it reasonable to expect them to detach themselves from this teleological vision? When one is situated in a context that prescribes a perspective wherein the whole is greater than the sum of its parts, such a dynamic impulse requires an organic, rather than a purely mechanistic, view of the total system. In this context, objective neutrality and subjective detachment become dysfunctional attributes of administrative behavior.

Finally, still another point concerning administrative neutrality needs to be addressed, if only in passing. It was noted earlier that when administrative neutrality becomes an end in itself, it "falls victim to the irony of unreality." This phrase was drawn from Dietrich Bonhoeffer, the German theologian who was hanged in a Nazi concentration camp in 1945, and it is especially relevant at this point that the phrase be presented in its original context: "A desire to be good for its own sake, as an end in itself, so to speak, or as a vocation in life, falls victim to the irony of unreality. The genuine striving for good now becomes the self-assertiveness of *the prig*."[28] Given this assertion, is it not reasonable to ask to what extent the "doctrine" of administrative neutrality gives way to administrative "priggishness"—that is to say, to an inflated sense of self-importance and self-regard, and, perhaps, even to an arrogant sense of self-righteousness?

The "doctrine" of administrative neutrality is, of course, encased in the notion of benevolence, as opposed to its opposite, malevolence. Moreover, the notions of benevolent disinterestedness and benign authority are recurrent themes in the history of civilization. If, however, one shifts to the history of administration, does not the very idea of a "benevolent disinterestedness" carry with it an implicit presumption of superiority? Is there not a supercilious tone that resonates in these verses:

> By lavish and progressive measures
> Our neighbor's wants are all relieved;
> We are not called to share his pleasures,
> And in his grief we are not grieved,[29]

and, then, are we not back in the midst of the Pharisees and scribes?

In other words, to what extent does the idea of administrative neutrality embody a notion of bureaucratic authority that, through its very expression, alienates public servants from the very purposes they are intended to serve? To what extent are these "powers" of neutral authority combined to create, as the critic and essayist Lionel Trilling would say,

> a Christ—but with none of the inconveniences of undertaking to intercede, of being a sacrifice, of reasoning with rabbis, of making sermons, of having disciples, of going to weddings and to funerals, of beginning something and at a certain point remarking that it is finished.[30]

Given such a myopic and attenuated democratic vision, administrative neutrality creates an artificial innocence that hardly serves the profession well. As the German philosopher Arthur Schopenhauer noted long ago,

> Innocence is in its very nature stupid. It is stupid because the aim of life ... is to gain a knowledge of our own bad will, so that our will may become an object for us, and that we may undergo an inward conversion.... In the state of innocence ... there is no evil because there is no experience.... The first criminal and murderer, Cain, who acquired a knowledge of guilt, and through guilt acquired a knowledge of virtue by repentance, and so came to understand the meaning of life, is a tragic figure more significant, and almost more respectable, than all the innocent fools in the world put together.[31]

A similar theme is reflected in the writings of the British novelist Graham Greene, who, incidentally, employed the motifs of public administration, especially duty and service, in many of his novels.

44

"Innocence," he wrote, "is like a dumb leper who has lost his bell, wandering the world, meaning no harm."[32]

Such a pretension of innocence results in imposing a heavy burden of hypocrisy most directly on the bureaucracy. To be sure, there are those who argue that the common thread in politics is hypocrisy, but, unlike the rain that falls on the good and bad alike, popularly elected executive and legislative officials seem particularly adept at ensuring that the public's perception of hypocrisy falls mainly on the career public servants. For example, what could be more innocently or neutrally perceived than the notion of tolerance? It is axiomatic that, in the American tradition, a high value is placed on tolerance. The fact remains, however, that, as public policy debates become increasingly focused on the omnipresent notion of "freedom of choice," the responsibility for managing the complexities of tolerance inevitably is delegated to the cadres of public servants. For those rare individuals in the bureaucracy who attempt to confront the manifold ethical-moral dilemmas inherent in these complex issues, there is the bleak prospect of being branded as intolerant enemies of freedom. Under these circumstances, prudence dictates, at least, a detached and dispassionate tolerance of tolerance. Thus, in the absence of support from top-level executive officials or Congress, the voices of our most experienced and knowledgeable administrators are silenced, and the scene is set for the play on hypocrisy. Viewed in this context, an observation by the British author Dorothy Sayers can be read as a grim commentary on our profession:

> In the world it calls itself toleration, but in hell it is called despair. . . . [Toleration] is the sin that believes in nothing, cares for nothing, seeks to know nothing, interferes with nothing, enjoys nothing, loves nothing, hates nothing, finds purpose in nothing, lives for nothing, and only remains alive because there is nothing it would die for.[33]

The pretense of innocence, of course, serves to reinforce this negative perception, and, for this reason, the artificial appearance of a duty in the name of service tends to project bureaucracy in its most unfavorable light. If this perception is to be changed in the years ahead, it is incumbent upon public servants, individually as professionals and collectively as a profession, to create a new reality for themselves—a new image that rings true of a service in the name of democracy.

To Play One's Part

There have been previous periods in history that have been preoccupied with dissimulation and pretense. As Lionel Trilling notes, "Dante had assigned those whose 'deeds were not of the lion but of the fox' to the penultimate circle of the Inferno, but Machiavelli reversed the judgment, at least in public life, by urging upon the Prince the way of the fox."[34] When the "great game of politics" is viewed literally as a game, the participants or actors assume roles to be played in accordance with rules that tend to favor the cunning, rather than the brave. In this context, the notion of pretense determines how one conducts oneself in the game or how one performs his or her role in the play. The gulf between intentions and actions can be vast as the British poet and critic Matthew Arnold so aptly reflects:

> Below the surface stream, shallow and light,
> Of what we *say* we feel—below the stream
> A light, of what we *think* we feel—there flows
> With noiseless current strong, obscure and deep,
> The central stream of what we feel indeed.[35]

To paraphrase the words spoken by Shakespeare's Timon of Athens, the public-sector administrator who becomes a craftsman of pretense is capable of making "black, white; fair, foul; / Wrong, right; base, noble; old, young; coward, valiant."[36]

The notion of pretense draws heavily from the ethical system of the Stoics and places great stress on one's ability "to play one's part." As the contemporary philosopher Alasdair MacIntyre notes, whenever "teleology, whether Aristotelian or Christian, is abandoned, there is always a tendency to substitute for it some version of Stoicism."[37] Operating out of this mold one would do well to recall the British novelist Jane Austen's description of Henry Crawford in

Mansfield Park, in which she captures the essence of the inauthentic self: "Whether it were dignity, or pride, or tenderness, or remorse, or whatever were to be expressed, he could do it with equal beauty. It was truly dramatic." To which Lionel Trilling adds in his commentary on the novel, "his adultery with Maria Bertram is not only loveless but lustless; so far from being forgivable as passion, a free expression of selfhood, it is merely a role undertaken, a part played as the plot requires."[38]

As we prepare to engage the twenty-first century, the predominant characteristic of public administration in America also appears to be not only loveless but lustless. The prevailing response, for example, to Vice-President Gore's *Report of the National Performance Review* appears to be that of a role undertaken, a part played as the plot requires, a renewed placement of the mask of hypocrisy. Given the model of public administration that was shaped in the formative years of our Republic, a pessimistic scenario for the twenty-first century can be derived from Perry Miller's description of the failed Puritan experiment. Using a familiar contemporary scene to frame his analogy, Miller observes:

> Year after year, as the circus tours this country, crowds howl with laughter, no matter how many times they have seen the stunt, at the bustle that walks by itself: the clown comes out dressed in a large skirt with a bustle behind; he turns sharply to the left, and the bustle continues blindly and obstinately straight ahead, on the original course. It is funny in a circus, but not in history. There is nothing but tragedy in the realization that one was in the main path of events, and now is sidetracked and disregarded. One is always able, of course, to stand firm on his first resolution, and to condemn the clown of history for taking the wrong turning: yet this is a desolate sort of Stoicism because it always carries with it the recognition that history will never come back to the predicted path, and that with one's own demise righteousness must die out in the world.[39]

There is, however, a more optimistic scenario that can be advanced based on the hope that the genuineness of the relationships that forges a democratic polity will cause our present administrative system to recall the sincerity and authenticity of the democratic vision it originally embraced. As suggested by Alasdair MacIntyre, it is in the framework of this democratic vision that

> We live out our lives, both individually and in our relationships with each other, in the light of certain conceptions of a possible shared future, a future in which certain conceptions beckon us forward and others repel us, some seem already foreclosed and others perhaps inevitable. There is no present which is not informed by some image of some future and an image of the future which always presents itself in the form of a telos—or of a variety of ends or goals—towards which we are either moving or failing to move in the present. Unpredictability and teleology therefore co-exist as part of our lives; like characters in a fictional narrative we do not know what will happen next, but nonetheless our lives have a certain form which projects itself towards our future. Thus ... it is always both the case that there are constraints on how the story can continue and that within those constraints there are indefinitely many ways that it can continue.[40]

We are all familiar with the efforts of the early Athenians to infuse the notion of democracy with an intrinsic sense of community as reflected in the concept of the *polis*. One cannot ignore, however, the complementary fact that for the early Greek Christians the concept of the *polis* was significantly transformed into the notion of *politeuma,* or the community of the coming age. To be sure, this latter concept reflected the central eschatological impulse of Christianity. Given this transformed perspective of the community and the future, however, do the *polis* and the *politeuma* become, like civilization and administration, two aspects of the same thing? Do they become fused to the notion of democracy? With the English settlement of America, were the colonists imbued with an eschatological vision? With the establishment of the Republic, did the Founding Fathers embrace democracy as the promise of a future community? As we begin a new century, is democracy perceived as the key to the optimistic hopefulness of the *good society?*

The answers to these questions can, in no small measure, be found in the linkages that have been forged over the past two centuries between the canons of bureaucracy and the constitutional visions of our democratic Republic. As discussed in the following chapter, the uniqueness of American bureaucracy is certainly not defined by the Constitution per se. Instead, its uniqueness is unmistakably defined by the character of our nation's democratic fabric. To comprehend the essence of bureaucracy in the United States one must, to be sure, recognize the growth of the Constitution, as reflected in the ever-expanding *corpus juris*. More to the point, however, the organic development of the nation's ethical-moral character, as reflected in the spirit of democracy, provides the more revealing insight. It is this theme that constitutes the primary focus of the following chapter.

3
Bureaucracy and the American Character

Shaping an Administrative System

Constitutional development in the United States obviously should be examined by a study of the law—the law as promulgated by Congress and as explicated by the Supreme Court. After all, we are a government of laws, not of men. In recognizing the obvious significance of these two branches of government in the developmental process of our democracy, however, it has been the role of the third branch of government, the executive branch, that has proven to be the most decisive in both positive and negative terms. To be sure, many of our presidents have assumed passive if not decidedly negative roles in defining and shaping the public policy process. Others have exerted a dynamic and positive impact on the process of constitutional development. Policy intentions, however, cannot be separated from policy implementation, and thus the growth of federal power in the United States can, in no small measure, be traced through the administrative apparatus of the federal executive branch.

Just as the president and other top-level policy officials (i.e., all political appointees) have been directed in active pursuit of or passive withdrawal from the impulse of national policy power, so, also, has the administrative cadre responsible for the implementation of policy demonstrated its own capabilities to enhance or impede the policy process. Clearly, Congress, the president, and the Supreme Court enjoy constitutional recognition; Articles I, II, and III focus explicitly on each. To ignore the policy role of the vaguely defined and amorphous body of career administrators known collectively as the "bureaucracy," however, is to ignore the critically important fourth player in an intensely competitive and intricately complex four-cornered game.

Admittedly, this assertion is based on over 200 years of cumulative experience. Although Jefferson, Hamilton, and Madison might be intrigued today by the twentieth-century developments of our three basic institutions—the presidency, Congress, and the Supreme Court—the Court would still be a recognizable body in a familiar setting; Congress would be larger—less eloquent, perhaps—but still the primary deliberative body, operating under familiar rules of parliamentary decorum; and the White House, despite its barricades, security forces, and banks of electronic wizardry, would still be at the other end of Pennsylvania Avenue. Could they comprehend the Departments of State, Health and Human Services, or Energy; the commissions, agencies, or government corporations; the complex networks of regional, district, and field offices; the intergovernmental systems or the transnational complex; the National Aeronautics and Space Administration? Given what the Framers collaborated to put into the Constitution concerning the administrative infrastructure of the executive branch, and given the overall sentiments that then prevailed concerning the role of bureaucracy in the new government, it seems reasonable to suggest that, from the Framers' perspective, the status of the bureaucracy today could only be viewed as phenomenal. The federal civil service, which totaled approximately 3,000 employees in 1800, is now numbered in the millions. How can such growth and complexity be explained in terms of the Constitution? Perhaps the best way to start is to let the Constitution and the intentions of its Framers speak for themselves.

A close reading of Article I, sections 6, 8, and 9, reveals that federal offices other than the president, vice-president, senators, representatives, and federal judges were anticipated; but the language is decidedly fuzzy, its focus hazy. Article II, section 2, is slightly more specific. There will be executive departments in the new government, but they are left unnamed and unnumbered. These departments will be directed by individuals who at one point in this section are referred to as "the principal Officer" and at a later point in the same section as "the Heads of Departments." These individuals shall be nominated and appointed by the president with the advice and consent of the Senate. Moreover, section 2 provides for "other . . . inferior Officers" who may be appointed, with prior congressional approval, directly by the president or by the heads of departments.

The key words used for structuring an administrative support system for the new government were executive departments, principal officers (heads of departments), and inferior officers. All else that has developed since the beginning of the Republic has been derived from these three terms. Upon reading Article II, one can truly begin to appreciate the astuteness of Alexis de Tocqueville, who perceived that the most amazing feature of our Constitution was "the variety of information and the amount of discernment that it presupposes in the people whom it is meant to govern."[1] This was a telling insight insofar as the administrative structure of the new government was concerned. Thus, with two important exceptions, the seeds of the federal bureaucracy can be found in the 224-word statement contained in Article II, section 2.

The first exception is contained in Article II, section 1: "The executive power shall be vested in a President of the United States of America." One could easily glide past this seemingly innocuous line were it not, as constitutional law scholar Edward Corwin reminded us, for the explosive potential that this simple declaratory sentence repressed.[2] In the first place, it settled the heated debate in the Constitutional Convention as to whether the chief executive was to be singular or plural in number. In the second place, it gave the holder of this position a precise title. The second exception is found in the next-to-last statement in Article II, section 3. Buried below a series of enumerated presidential clerkship duties can be found what Hamilton would have described as the source of the energetic impulse of the presidency and of the entire executive branch: "[H]e shall take Care that the Laws be faithfully executed."

One can only wonder why this operative phrase was not linked to the opening sentence of Article II. The result would have been a dynamic, action-forcing statement: "The executive Power shall be vested in a President of the United States of America [who] shall take Care that the Laws be faithfully executed." Certainly by linking the two intentions together and by positioning them prominently at the beginning of Article II, the office and its primary function could have been strategically emphasized. Some clue to this disjunctive phrasing can be gained by reference to a debate that arose in the drafting of Article II.

During the draft stage, Madison suggested wording that explicitly identified the establishment of a Department of Foreign Affairs headed by an individual "to be called the Secretary of the Department of Foreign Affairs who shall be appointed by the President with advice and consent of the Senate, and to be removable by the President."[3] The Framers could not agree on this clause, so the Madisonian crispness was replaced by the more generally acceptable fuzziness of Article I, section 2.

That the Constitution speaks to the bureaucratic support structure of the new government in *sotto voce* is no accident. Instead, it reflects a logical solution to the kind of group decision making we have all experienced. That is, when dealing with primary issues of major significance, avoid controversies over secondary issues that can subvert agreement on the former. This is particularly true if the secondary issues involve elements that are so obvious that they do not have to be made explicit. As split as the fifty-five Framers may have been on the fundamental issues and methods of governance, the necessity for some kind of administrative cadre was taken as a given. The scope and magnitude of the new government was a debatable issue, but law in action was administration, and there was certainly no question that the new regime would promulgate laws. Hence, the necessity for an administrative support staff was a nondebatable issue. It was an obvious fact of political life.

Bear in mind that the historical reality and necessity for "inferior officers" were well established by 1787. For the preceding 150 years, America was internally administered by colonists working in the service of either the colonial governors or the colonial legislatures. As the colonies grew in number and size, policymaking became more complex just as administrative practices became more permanent. As political scientist Robert Goldwin reminded us several years ago, "considering how long Americans were on this continent before 1787, it is perfectly intelligent to speak of what the American constitution was before the Constitution of the United States was written."[4] One important part of that colonial American character involved the administrative implementation of policy intentions. Clearly, this caused various individuals to become involved in administrative methods, techniques, organizational structures, rules, and procedures. It may not be fair to say that in 1787 the new government "hit the ground running" on this issue of an administrative support staff, but it certainly did not have to start from point zero.

Leonard White, the eminent historian of American public admin-istration, argues that while the art of self-government flourished dur-ing the colonial period, the craft of management hardly existed. Moreover, he notes that the art of evading government assumed ma-jor proportions, becoming something of a "high art."[5] Perhaps White's standards are set too high. To judge that which passed as ad-ministrative implementation by the canons of management is some-what unreasonable. Public management as a science was beginning to take formidable shape in Europe at this time, and the administra-tive form that emerged in the colonies certainly paled by compari-son. Nevertheless, colonial budgets were put together, records were kept, public projects were undertaken, and public order was main-tained. Was all of this carried out with managerial artistry? no; with administrative sufficiency? unquestionably, yes.

Certainly by 1787 the development of colonial administration had progressed to the point where a body of experience had devel-oped beyond the primitive stage. Moreover, one should not overlook the fact that administrative experience was not derived solely from the public sector. The successful operation of banks, businesses, and even large farms required some degree of administrative skill and competent judgment, even if manifested in rather unsophisticated and elementary form. For example,

> Symbolic of the state of the administrative art in early American business was the preference for committees rather than single ex-ecutives. The directors of the Massachusetts Bank confided even the smallest matters to committees of the board—the alteration and repair of the building, the procurement of a bell in case of fire or robbery, the erecting of a lightning rod. . . . The direct su-pervision of banking transactions was the duty of a "sitting direc-tor" selected in turn by the alphabet, to be in charge for a week.[6]

In addition to the cumulative body of experience gained from the colonial years that caused the administrative function to be taken for granted in the Constitution, the experience derived from the Continental Congress and the Articles of Confederation was also in-structive. The constitutional reference to "departments" has to be read in light of the fact that, under the Articles of Confederation, Departments of Foreign Affairs, Treasury, War, Navy, and the Post Office had been established and their continuation seemed prudent. Similarly, the genesis of the terms "principal Officer" and "Heads of Departments" can also be traced to the experience obtained under the Articles. For instance, committees of the Continental Congress initially attempted to perform directly the administrative functions of the established departments, but the committee members were quick to realize the heavy burden of carrying out both legislative and administrative functions. Private citizens were then selected and organized into boards accountable to the Continental Congress to perform the implementation function. Operational ineffectiveness, however, continued to persist. Under these plural bodies, considerable time was lost, and administrative efficiency was seldom even closely approximated. Thus, the next logical step was to create the position of secretary to serve as the principal operating officer of each department. Just as it was assumed that the departmental structure would be carried over into the new government, it was also assumed that each would be headed by a principal officer known as the secretary.[7]

Thus, the new Republic was launched, complete with the basic elements of an administrative system, and while it cannot be said that this bureaucratic enterprise flourished, neither can it be said that it floundered. Indeed, the policy and administrative challenges were formidable, and although the demands and responsibilities for running a nation were, in 1787 as in the present, endeavors that dwarfed all others by comparison, the values of individual initiative, courage, and self-responsibility were the dominant expressions of the newly formed administrative class. For those who entered the public sector, these values served as a base on which operational competency was subsequently developed. The new government was infused with intentions and moved by actions; purpose clearly preceded process. The intentions were explicitly value based; the purpose was viewed as a transcendent common good, fuzzily defined but intuitively felt.

Both the original set of intentions and the original sense of purpose are viewed by many today as quaint and prosaic remnants of our past, ill suited to meet the complex challenges of the twenty-first century. The almost linear decline of such sublime faith and hope in the administrative mission is, we are told, inversely related to the seemingly linear rise of a politicized bureaucracy that extended through most of the nineteenth century. Such a view does not lack persuasive evidence, but such evidence is not without a competing counterforce. Throughout the nineteenth-century cycle of political degeneration, one can also trace the persistent strain of a commitment to those eloquent values that yielded a deeply entrenched faith in a transcendent good. Both sets of these contradictory values infused the spirit of bureaucracy as it matured during those formative years. Both sets of values are central to an understanding of our particular bureaucratic-democratic ethos and need to be examined in some detail.

The Jacksonian Imprint

When Andrew Jackson began his presidency in 1829, he inherited what he perceived to be an impossible, schizophrenic bureaucracy. The first twelve years of the Republic were carried out under the governance of the Federalists. The artful guidance of George Washington yielded a fairly high degree of operational cohesion with a relatively low degree of ideological fervor. This attitude, however, did not prevail for long. Policy and political differences, often bitter and intense, started to divide the nation into Federalist and Antifederalist camps, and in 1801, with the election of Jefferson, the spirit and tone of democracy began to reflect a notably different tenor than that which had characterized the Federalist years. From 1801 to 1829, the policy and programmatic intentions of Jeffersonian Republicans contrasted sharply with those of the Federalists, and the two periods—one of twelve years' duration and the other of twenty-eight—must be viewed as philosophically and politically discrete. Viewed in terms of specific programmatic policy activity, however, the two periods were much less sharply delineated; more significantly, the administrative apparatus established at the outset by the Federalists remained essentially intact during the entire forty-year period. Thus, when Jackson entered office in 1829, he inherited a policy philosophy infused with the values of Jeffersonian republicanism. He also incurred a forty-year heritage of Federalist values deeply embedded in a substantially enlarged administrative structure. Jackson found the tenets of Jeffersonian republicanism essentially congenial to his own way of thinking, but he viewed the Federalist values, revealed in the administrative structure, as a totally unwarranted and illegitimate subversion, not only of his own brand of democratic republicanism, but of his constitutionally imposed responsibility to ensure that the laws be faithfully executed.

Paradoxically, Jackson's views of presidential leadership were much more akin to those of Hamilton than those of Jefferson, and Jackson's presidency provided a benchmark in the emergence of a strong, forceful, and dynamic chief executive. Aside from this stylist link to the Federalists, Jackson's personal ethical-moral values were reflected in the spirit of a new democracy that was totally antithetical to the Federalist perspective. As a consequence, Jackson provided our constitutional and political history with not one but two lasting imprints: a model of a strong chief executive and the champion spokesman for the democratization of the public service, that is, the federal bureaucracy.

The infusion of a new "publicness" into the spirit and mechanics of democratic government, which started with Jackson, extended more than fifty years to the administration of Cleveland (excluding, of course, the Civil War years). Depending on one's predilections, it was a period that could be characterized as the Dark Ages of American government. As noted in chapter 1, Congress, the presidency, the administrative branch, and the courts were all scarred and scathed by the partisan political holocaust that swept through the nation—the spoils system. In the name of a new spirit of democracy, the federal establishment became politicized to the point where, democratic values aside, the basic notions of human decency were placed in grave jeopardy of survival.

As early as 1868, *The Nation*, one of the country's leading politically focused magazines, editorialized:

> With a Constitution purified from slavery, with a government under it that has undergone the throes of civil war, of dissensions, between its coordinate branches, and with a people honestly and heartily in earnest to maintain both the government and the Constitution, there is still a vice in the administration of the laws

which almost palsies them. This mischief lies in the shifting, changing, uncertain, and gradually decaying conditions of our civil service.[8]

On the eve of the 1880 presidential election, in which James A. Garfield emerged victorious, *The Nation* was still searching for "an honest and generally efficient and business-like conduct of the departments without scandal of jobbery." Again the editors urged action that would prevent

> eighty thousand officers and their families from retiring at night with much the same feelings as the inhabitants of a besieged city who know that in the morning their homes may be given up to pillage if the defense should not hold out. Such a quadrennial terror we have called an Oriental barbarism, and no human man will contend that it ought to be perpetuated, or that Republican or Democratic Executive Committees should be allowed to play on it, on the twofold pretense, first, that the party is the country, and, second, that the civil service is an appanage of party.[9]

The true significance of the contributions by the Federalist administrative system to the stability and the civility of the democratic policy process became visibly apparent when compared to that which stood in its place some fifty years later. The purported elitist criteria of the Federalist notions of public service were abandoned in favor of political endorsements. The notion of career permanence was rejected in favor of rotation in office. The idea of professional expertise was dismissed in favor of political loyalty. The concept of a *civil* service was discounted in favor of partisan incivility. Each of these factors, it must be emphasized, represented the manifest tendencies and general inclinations evidenced in government at the time. Although they were not the only forces that prevailed, their overall effects and the concomitant values they manifested had a decidedly negative impact on the administrative system.

Viewed objectively, the period was predominantly a disaster for the career public service, with one important exception. During this period, national expansion and complexity accelerated in virtually every dimension, and as the nation expanded dramatically in both population and area, the federal administrative apparatus was forced to expand as well. Jackson was no nationalist; but national expansion, as Jefferson and his cohorts were quick to learn, could not be abated or ignored. If the Constitution follows the flag, can the bureaucracy be far behind?

Although Jackson was dogmatic in his vision of a strong chief executive, the power he attempted to centralize was designed to guard against government control, rather than to extend federal policy regulation. Throughout the Jacksonian period, and beyond, "the strongest argument in justification of broad constitutional powers in the federal government was aimed at preventing regulation by the state."[10] According to President Van Buren, such a laissez-faire government would "leave every citizen and every interest to reap under its benign protection the rewards of virtue, industry, and prudence."[11] In keeping with this attitude, President Pierce vetoed, in 1854, a bill that authorized the granting of public lands to the states for the benefit of indigent insane persons.[12] Pierce reasoned that to extend such preferential treatment would logically lead to extending the same consideration to the indigent but sane, and he refused to move the federal government in that direction. Pierce, however, was not without a charitable bent. From 1850 to 1857 he joined forces with his predecessor, President Fillmore, to sign into law the appropriation of 25 million acres of federal public land to the states for the construction of more than fifty railroads. Indeed, as a result of this policy decision to utilize public lands for the enhancement of the private sector, Congressman Justin Morrill was prompted to introduce his land-grant college bill that would transfer federal lands to the states as an incentive for the construction of state universities. Morrill's measure passed both the House and the Senate in 1857. On this issue, however, it was President Buchanan, not Pierce, who had to make the tough decision. His veto endorsed, as "undeniable," the proposition "that Congress does not possess the power to appropriate money ... for the purposes of educating the people of the respective states."[13] In the post–Civil War years, President Grant was, at one point, inclined to use federal funds to alleviate the depression of 1874 through the means of proto WPA projects. James Garfield, then a congressman, and Grant's secretary of the treasury, Benjamin H. Bristow, convinced him to reconsider such a perilous policy. When Garfield became president, he subsequently announced that "it was not part of the functions of the national government to fund employment for people." This attitude carried through to President Cleveland, who noted, in connection with the economic recessions that plagued his administration, "that while the people should patriotically and cheerfully support their government, its functions do not include the support of the people."[14]

The period of constitutional and political history covering the pre–Civil War Jacksonian democracy and the post–Civil War republicanism began on a note of high-spirited democratic humanism. It progressively degenerated, however, into an ugly mood of political nihilism and social despair. In the waning decades of the nineteenth century, the federal regulatory power did begin to assert itself, but only slowly. The objective reality of the corrupting effects of unregulated social complexity reflected the complementary emphasis of the social Darwinism of the English philosopher Herbert Spencer, the Protestant ethic of Calvinism, and the "invisible hand" of the Scottish political economist Adam Smith. The federal administrative system was pulled into the vicious vortex of these countervailing forces, and although it was not crushed, it emerged from the vise badly bruised. Caught in the midst of a turbulent social reality that was fundamentally altering the American character from rural agrarianism to urban industrialism, and a turbulent political reality that was fundamentally altering the democratic character from the artistry of citizen participation to the craftiness of citizen manipulation, the federal bureaucracy was much more the victim than the victimizer. And yet, despite the predominant mood of political corruption that pervaded the federal establishment, the noble side of the democratic spirit of bureaucracy was never completely snuffed out. Perhaps goodness, in the form of energetic courage, initiative, and self-responsibility, is the sine qua non of a constitutional democracy and a democratic bureaucracy. On the other hand, perhaps such characteristics are evidenced solely on the basis of chance. In any event, the nineteenth century was not a total wasteland as far as the growth of bureaucratic competence, wisdom, and virtue was concerned.

The Pursuit of Happiness

Viewing the foundation established by the early Federalists, the distinguished American historians Samuel Morison and Henry Steele Commager observed, "seldom has a class acted more wisely for the good of the whole than the Federalists."[15] Integrity and firmness became the guiding principles of President Washington, and he bequeathed good faith and justice to the nation in his Farewell Address. Even the Antifederalist Jefferson pressed for a trained cadre of career officials endowed by "genius and virtue." Although Washington may have been the guardian of Federalist democracy and Jefferson may have been democracy's republican prophet, it was the Father of American Transcendentalism, Ralph Waldo Emerson, who became democracy's high priest. Moving beyond Jefferson, Emerson sought to expose the existential being of democracy. Thus, it was Emerson, not Jefferson, who saw that free institutions would never liberate a body politic that was not, itself, free of blind prejudice, hatred, and corruption—that is, not free to think out the full consequences of democracy.[16] As Morison and Commager noted, Emerson's "Transcendentalism was a movement to liberate America spiritually, as independence and democracy had liberated her politically; an attempt to make Americans worthy of their independence and elevate them to a new stature among mortals."[17]

By the same token, however, it was probably Jefferson, rather than Emerson, who had the better insight into the inherent nature of the American character. The neat and orderly rationalism that served to frame Emerson's transcendentalism could hardly have fit into Jefferson's more pragmatic republican idealism. To paraphrase an analogy offered by a Federalist member of the first Congress, Fisher Ames, transcendentalism "is like a merchantman. You get on board and ride the wave and tide in safety and elation but, by and by, you strike a reef and go down. But democracy is like a raft. You never sink but, dammit, your feet are always in the water."[18]

To keep the raft afloat required hard work, ingenuity, common sense, and a high degree of personal integrity—characteristics much more closely associated with the pragmatic deists of the early Federalist period than with the transcendental Unitarians who followed. Democracy's prophet and high priest together inspired the new Republic and infused its theoretical underpinnings with a sense of moral consciousness, but the craftsmanship of governmental operations was drawn more directly from the practical wisdom of Benjamin Franklin than from either Jefferson, the prophet, or Emerson, the high priest. Indeed, the imprint of Franklin was stamped deep on the psyche of the federal bureaucracy from the very beginnings of its operation. Hard work, ingenuity, common sense, and personal integrity were the fundamental values employed in the administrative implementation of public policy.

As stated in chapter 2, Washington reflected this practical wisdom when he commented: "We now have a National character and it is of the utmost importance to stamp favorable impressions upon it." As president, he strove to transform this principle into action: "In every nomination to office I have endeavored . . . to make fitness of character my primary objective."[19] During the early years of the Republic the notion of fitness of character, however badly it may have been abused in the subsequent years, was, nevertheless, consistently evidenced in the forms of administrative virtue, integrity, and firmness. Hamilton, as secretary of the treasury, set the early benchmark for administrative vision and wisdom. During the period from 1817 to 1825, the War Department, under the direction of John C. Calhoun, replaced the Treasury Department as the dynamic center of government operations.[20] The high standards of integrity, responsibility, and accountability imposed by Calhoun on his subordinates were duplicated by John McLean, who served as postmaster general from 1823 to 1829. Moreover, for each of these three early department heads, policy implementation was viewed in a positive and dynamic context. Hamilton and Calhoun undoubtedly would have concurred with McLean when he observed: "I say now as I have always said on the subject, that I do not consider an efficient administration of the department is shown by an annual balance in its favor. Its funds should be actively employed in extending the operations of the mail."[21]

Clearly, the first forty years of the new Republic were shaped by the gentlemanly public service values of the Federalist tradition. The dismal pockmarks of the political corruption that infected the nation during the remaining years of the nineteenth century, however, were offset, in part, by putting the old elixir in a new bottle. George

Bancroft, as secretary of the navy under President Polk, wrote that he would be guided by two maxims: "First, regard to the public service; and second, to act as if the eye of the whole democracy watched every motion and its ear heard every word I shall utter. Duty and publicity will be my watchwords."[22] A strong sense of publicness infused the Treasury Department again when President Pierce appointed James Guthrie as its secretary. Honesty, integrity, vigilance, fidelity, and economy were the guiding virtues employed by Guthrie, who, according to Leonard White, took to his task "with all the zeal of a ruthless reformer." As seen by Guthrie, the public was to be treated by all Treasury employees with frankness, courtesy, and kindness. "Thus, by dignity of deportment and an accommodating spirit, [each clerk would] serve to conciliate ... the confidence and respect of the people for the government."[23] Moreover, other basic public-service values such as expertise and responsiveness were incorporated in an emerging new professionalism that was located in the newly created Department of Agriculture.

Organized originally in 1862 as a subcabinet department headed by a commissioner, and elevated to full cabinet status in 1889,* this department was destined to become the trendsetter for many of the

---

* The establishment of the U.S. Department of Agriculture with full cabinet status in 1889 followed a nearly 100-year gestation period. In the early days of the Republic, when the Patent Office was part of the State Department, the Commissioner of Patents was designated as the receiving clerk for all exotic seed and cuttings that American consuls in distant lands were instructed to send back to the United States. This obviously industrious and imaginative federal clerk, operating only on a State Department directive and with no funds, enlisted the cooperative support of various congressmen who began distributing free seeds to their constituents. In time, this makeshift operation began to flourish and, in 1839, Congress made its first $1,000 appropriation for seed distribution, agricultural research, and the gathering of agricultural statistics. In 1849, the Patent Office was transferred to the newly created Interior Department but still maintained responsibility for this mini-agriculture "program." In 1862, the "program" was transferred to the newly established subcabinet Department of Agriculture, by which time the annual appropriations for agricultural activities, including the free seed program, had expanded to $60,000. See Swisher, *American Constitutional Development,* 367–77; and White, *Republican Era,* 238.

best (and some of the less-than-best) features of our bureaucratic-democratic ethos. From its beginning, the department was permeated with a sense of mission that White describes as an undercurrent of devotion to the qualitative improvement of farm life in particular and to human life in general. Deeply steeped in political astuteness from the outset, the department, nonetheless, was predominantly concerned with science, not politics; with experimental programs, not partisan campaigning; and with long-range planning, not immediate payoffs.[24]

Agriculture was the first client-oriented department in the federal establishment, but it was also the first science-oriented department. These two conditions combined very nicely to serve the steadily expanding regulatory inclinations of Congress. Unlike the Departments of the Treasury, War, or Post Office, for example, which were organized around clerks engrossed in the implementation of highly structured, routinized program activity, the Agriculture Department, with its cadre of highly diversified scientists, was effectively utilized in countless ways to extend the constitutional presence of the federal government into virtually every hamlet in the nation. To be sure, in the twilight years of the nineteenth century, the expansion of federal regulatory policy was certainly not limited to the mandates assigned the Department of Agriculture by Congress.[25] The patterns of federal regulatory activity associated with the independent regulatory commissions, for example, differed significantly from those assigned to the Agriculture Department. Nevertheless, it is important to note that the portents of the positive state, which emerged full force in 1933, are not to be found in the value assumptions that infused the independent regulatory commissions; instead, they are to be found in the public service commitment that pervaded the Department of Agriculture.

The tone and tenor of this commitment were set quite simply, but explicitly, by the department's first full-fledged secretary, Jeremiah Rusk: "Everything that leads to a more intimate acquaintance between the department and the farmers throughout the country must be mutually advantageous."[26] It is doubtful that any of the early Federalists would have concurred with a literal rendering of Rusk's pronouncement. There can be no doubt, however, that their respective purposeful intentions would have been the same. The administrative vision of a transcendent purpose could apply equally to both periods, with traces being consistently revealed throughout the interim years. Indeed, the sense of administrative ethics that wends its way through our constitutional history suggests a norm of material life that has been consistently portrayed in art, literature, and the Bible. In Shakespeare's play *The Tempest* (IV, i), Ferdinand speaks of the hope of "quiet days, fair issue, and long life," a theme that is repeated by Juno in the same scene: "Honor, riches, marriage blessing / Long continuance and increasing / ... Earth's increase, foison plenty / Barns and garners never empty." Citing these passages, Lionel Trilling notes that "it has to do with good harvests and full barns and the qualities of affluent decorum."[27] This same symbol of virtue is reflected in the Book of Proverbs in the form of a simple causal proposition: "[If you] Honor the Lord with your substance and with the first fruits of all you produce, then your barns will be filled with plenty and your vats will be bursting with wine."[28]

The idea of prosperity was linked to freedom in forming a key element of our democratic heritage, and although the Founding Fathers were not unmindful of a material prosperity associated with good harvests and full barns, Jefferson's notion of the pursuit of happiness (linked though it can be to Locke's notion of property) does suggest a prosperity that is much more normative and spiritual in its symbolic content. The Greek concept of *eudaemonism*, or happiness, when combined with the biblical notion of obligation (Honor the Lord) becomes, in our democratic ethos, the foundation from which virtue is derived. The pursuit of happiness, along with the freedoms of life and liberty, will yield good harvests and full barns; but they also will yield a spiritual and an ethical plentitude that will ensure a government designed solely in response to the needs and wants of the governed. To paraphrase Jeremiah Rusk, an intimate acquaintance must bind government and the governed— and especially the bureaucracy and the citizenry.

The notion of intimate acquaintance suggests an element of sincerity, and the richness gained from sincerely founded interpersonal relationships creates a prosperity of happiness that becomes energized by an inner sense of obligation. Thus, as a result of this deeply rooted sense of happiness and obligation, the abject political immorality generated by the spoils system that threatened the inner nucleus of democracy was never totally successful in destroying the integrity that was inherent in the sound craftsmanship of public administration, particularly as that craft was applied in its bureaucratic-democratic form. In its many subsequent manifestations—whether energized by the tenets of scientific management, partisan mutual adjustment, or analytical optimization—the operational competence of public administration has always been held accountable to the more fundamental and transcendent values of our bureaucratic-democratic tradition. As Abigail Adams long ago advised her young son, John Quincy, "Great learning and superior abilities, should you ever possess them, will be of little value and small estimation unless virtue, honor, truth, and integrity are added to them."[29] What can be learned from this experience is that unyielding individual integrity, moral rectitude, and ethical maturity—the core elements of a democratic ethos—cannot be taken for granted. Instead, they have to be applied, practiced, and cultivated—nurtured and nourished—in a purposeful environment that is conducive to the free and open—the unashamed and unabashed—expression of such values.

The effects of Jacksonian democracy and partisan politics on the federal administrative complex were many and varied, but one seemingly paradoxical pattern appeared most pronounced. In both centripetal and centrifugal fashion, the federal bureaucracy was simultaneously pulled *into* the body politic as a result of the politicized nature of the public service, and driven *away* from the body politic as a result of the prevailing laissez-faire philosophy of public policy. Ironically, these counteracting forces provided the fertile seedbed for the subsequent growth of a democratized merit system on the one hand, and the clearly demarcated policy-administration and value-fact dichotomies on the other.

The political reform movement that swept across the nation during the closing decades of the nineteenth century became fixed on the concepts of procedural fairness, equity, and impartiality, and, in no small measure, the impressive organizational achievements of the Department of Agriculture significantly influenced the thrust of this reform movement. Unfortunately, however, only half of the department's success formula was embraced: the lustrous brilliance of an undiluted, undefiled, and unadulterated science of management became the new hope of the twentieth-century policy process. In this instance, however, that which was overlooked proved to be much more important than that which was embraced, and the words of Abigail Adams assumed even greater prophetic proportions: "Great learning and superior abilities ... will be of little value and small estimation unless virtue, honor, truth, and integrity are added to them."

The science of agriculture was immutably linked to a critically conscious sense of a salutary public mission. This resulted in the emergence of an ethics of responsible citizenship. By contrast, the science of management that evolved in the federal bureaucracy during the first third of the twentieth century was linked to the notion of detached objectivity, as discussed previously in the opening chapter. The administration of public policy during this period was driven, as Max Weber would say, *sine ira ac studio*—without passion or enthusiasm. And, once again from the past, we hear the transcendental whispers of Ralph Waldo Emerson reminding us that nothing great was ever achieved without enthusiasm.

Does Administration Have a Soul?

What emerges from this all-too-brief examination of the development of our nation's administrative system during the nineteenth century is a combination of elements that somehow must be captured and linked together to form the essence of a bureaucratic ethic consistent with, and supportive of, the basic tenets of our democratic creed. Learning, in the form of intellectual competency; virtue, in the form of ethical maturity and moral integrity; and enthusiasm, in the form of purposeful democratic objectives are all essential elements that form the basis of an effective bureaucratic system. Such effectiveness, however, cannot be derived in a vacuum or on a unilateral basis; it can be developed and maintained only on the basis of reciprocal relationships.

First, policy impulses must flow reciprocally between career administrators and policy officials; second, such impulses must also flow reciprocally between career administrators and the citizenry. Thus, the infusion and expansion of intellectual capabilities, ethical maturity, moral integrity, and democratic purposefulness are possible only where interpersonal relationships are marked by some common bond. Indeed, in regard to all three of these sets of participants in the policy process—policy officials, career bureaucrats, and individual citizens—reciprocal lines must be drawn linking each to the others in a common bond of trust and loyalty. Such trust and loyalty form the basis of a constitutional faithfulness that is the generative source of an intellectual, ethical, and purposeful interdependence between policy officials, career bureaucrats, and individual citizens.

As reflected in the Book of Proverbs, loyalty and faithfulness are two of the basic biblical themes that permeate our entire democratic tradition: "Let not loyalty and faithfulness forsake you; bind them around your neck, write them on the tablet of your heart."[30] From the Greeks, loyalty and faithfulness to authority were reflected in the notions of *hieras* ("sacred") and *archos* ("leader") from which was derived the early Christian concept of *hierarchia* ("hierarchy") and *hierarches* ("one who is a hierarch"). Similarly, it was also from the early Christians that the notion of love was given a specific theological connotation that served to bind all citizens, regardless of official rank or social position, into a common fellowship based on the reciprocity of loyalty and faithfulness. This loyalty and faithfulness, as encapsulated in the notion of love of God and love of neighbor, is the dominant theme of the New Testament and is subsequently reflected in our own democratic tradition in the form of Jefferson's social ethic. Life, liberty, and the pursuit of happiness are totally vacuous concepts unless viewed in terms of the loyalty and faithfulness to a love that binds citizen to citizen, neighbor to neighbor. What can be derived from biblical tradition is a holistic synthesis of loyalty *and* faithfulness, obligation *and* love, purpose *and* being; and it is just such a synthesis that is reflected in the democratic ethos that permeates our constitutional character.

Perhaps it is too much to suggest that this is exactly what Hamilton, Jefferson, and Madison had in mind as they guided the formation of our Constitution and subsequently lent their efforts to the actual responsibilities of making the new government work. It is certainly not too much to suggest, however, that, despite their radically different perspectives of the central government's policy and regulatory responsibilities, as well as the role of the federal bureaucracy in carrying out these tasks, they were in complete accord that the intrinsic elements needed to make a constitutional democracy work were essentially ethical and moral in character. Viewed in terms of democratic theory and political rhetoric, this intrinsic ethical and moral "goodness" of the American character has never escaped our attention over the past 200 years. Nevertheless, the paths that guide theory and rhetoric, on the one hand, and actual day-to-day operational decisions, on the other, have diverged more frequently than they have converged over the same period. The major premise advanced here is that the critical variable affecting the degree of convergence or divergence between these forces (i.e., theory and practice, or intentions and acts, or policy and administration, or even morality and ethics) is the role assumed by the federal bureaucracy in the policy process.

Some years ago, Norton Long wrote: "Accustomed as we are to the identification of election with both representation and democracy, it seems strange at first to consider that the nonelected civil service may be both more representative of the country and more democratic in its composition than Congress."[31] On the surface, this proposition appears to rest solely on an empirical base, and it would be totally unwarranted to suggest that Long intended any conclusion other than the empirical observation he advanced. Nevertheless, if Long's observation is juxtaposed with another more avowedly normative proposition advanced by the political scientist David Levitan more than fifty years ago, an interesting ethical speculation concerning the role of bureaucracy in our constitutional system can be advanced. "An outstanding government administrator once remarked," Levitan wrote,

> that "administration must have a soul." ... It needs to be added, however, that administration should contribute to the fuller development of the soul of the state ... that a democratic state must be not only based on democratic principles but also democratically administered ... that administrative procedures are more important in effectuating the basic principles of government than is substantive law; and that these procedures must therefore be constantly reexamined in terms of the ends they serve and changed when the changing social and economic milieu requires different means to attain these ends.[32]

The notion that "administration must have a soul" is an interesting proposition despite its confounding implications. In the medieval merger of church and state, the imprint of the human soul became a matter of central significance when the Divine Right of Kings doctrine, complete with papal anointment, carried with it not only the divinely ordained right to rule but also the divinely ordained responsibility for the protection of even the lowest vassal. Ostensibly, the Reformation cleaved a nominal dichotomy between church and state, and the Enlightenment cut an even deeper swath between the metaphysical and physical worlds. As a result, concern about divinely ordained responsibility for human worth presumably could be ignored by all purely secular political institutions.

In actual fact, of course, we know this was not to be the case. The nation-state, from its emergence to the present day—and that is to say *every* nation-state—has been forced to address this immutable and implacable concept. As ingeniously as it has attempted for the past 500 years to finesse the theological implications of this concept, no nation-state has been able to ignore the ontological system of ethics associated with the notion of human worth or being. Our own revolutionary document, the Declaration of Independence, rests on the premise that the divinely ordained soul of a people had been profaned by a despotic and tyrannical king. Moreover, in anticipating the Preamble to the Constitution, the Declaration of Independence concludes by "appealing to the Supreme Judge of the world for the rectitude of our intentions."

If the notion of the human soul comes to us from the Greeks as filtered through the Christianity of the Middle Ages, still another theological concept relates directly to our democratic experience, namely, the New Testament's Greek notion of love (*agape*) as reflected also in the Latin (*caritas*). From ancient Rome, the concepts of citizen and citizenship flow forward to form the underpinnings of the U.S. Constitution. It is, however, the notion of *caritas* that was certainly seen by Jefferson as creating a democracy not just of the people, by the people, for the people, as Lincoln phrased it, but a democracy always of one individual self related to another individual self through the impulse of neighborly love. Indeed, the democratic character of America incorporates both concepts in the sense of a love or deep and genuine respect for the intrinsic dignity shared among fellow citizens. Thus, although all of our chief executives, legislators, and jurists are sworn to uphold this implicit premise of our constitutional system, it is the career public servants—the bureaucracy—who are most directly and personally confronted by its challenge. Viewed in this context, Levitan's provocative observation—"administration should contribute to the fuller development of the soul of the state"—can begin to assume practical significance.

For example, as cited by Leonard White, such an attitude was expressed in the very early years of our Republic by one unidentified writer who observed:

> Good government manifestly depends much more on the goodness of the men who fill the public offices, than on the goodness of the form of government, constitution, or even laws of the state; for the errors of all these, under the administration of good men, will be mended or made tolerable ... but weak and wicked men will pervert the best laws to the purposes of favour or oppression.[33]

A similar attitude was also reflected by Jefferson, who observed that "on great occasions every good officer must be ready to risk himself in going beyond the strict line of the law when the public preservation requires it; his motives will be a justification."[34] Later, following the purchase of the Louisiana Territory, Jefferson found the need to apply his own advice to himself, and his response was resoundingly eloquent.

> The legislature, in casting behind them metaphysical subtleties and risking themselves like faithful servants, must ratify and pay for it, and must throw themselves on their country for doing for them unauthorized what we know they would have done for themselves had they been in a situation to do it. It is the case of a guardian investing the money of his ward in purchasing an important adjacent territory, and saying to him when of age, I did this for your good; I pretend to no right to bind you; you may disavow me and I must get out of the scrape as best I can. I thought it my duty to risk myself for you.[35]

"I thought it my duty to risk myself for you." With these words Jefferson illuminated the intrinsic link between policy implementation and a deep affection and respect—or, simply, love—for the sanctity of democracy. This sense of responsibility was reflected by Secretary of the Navy George Bancroft, when he said that "duty and publicity will be my watchwords"; by Secretary of the Treasury James Guthrie, who insisted that frankness, courtesy, and kindness be extended to the public by his clerks with a dignity of deportment and an accommodating spirit; and by Secretary of Agriculture Jeremiah Rusk, who proclaimed that "everything that leads to a more intimate acquaintance between the department and the farmers . . . must be mutually advantageous."

From these comments, one can, perhaps, glean just what is involved in assuming the duty of risk in the administrative implementation of public policy. At the least, it means incurring practical risks by demonstrating initiative in creative, imaginative, and innovative problem solving. It certainly means incurring ethical risks associated with openness, sharing, trust, and loyalty. Conversely, however, it means guarding carefully against the dangerous political risks of excessive zeal and blind obedience. As Herman Finer, in citing the French political philosopher Montesquieu, sternly inveighs, "his phrase deserves to be put into the center of every discussion of administrative responsibility, *virtue itself hath need of limits*. We in public administration must beware of the too good man as well as the too bad."[36]

Given the very serious consequences associated with risk taking, perhaps we should be wary of urging our bureaucratic cadres to risk themselves for us in the name of democracy. History provides too many examples of administrative villainy borne in the cradle of virtuousness. Thus, our constitutional tradition strongly emphasizes the notion that ours is a government of laws, not of men; responsible constitutional democracy is founded on rational collective deliberation and not on impetuous individual risk taking.

The Sense of Duty

Given the emphasis placed on administrative responsibility and accountability, risk taking by nonelected public servants does constitute a valid concern. The fact remains, however, that the luster of our precious democratic concepts can also be corroded by an administrative service that has been intellectually, ethically, and motivationally neutered by the canons of objective impersonality in the name of efficiency, economy, impartiality, or procedural justice. The sense of authentic mission that characterized much of the nineteenth-century bureaucratic experiment was, to be sure, grossly contorted and corrupted by the machinations of an ogreish patronage system. Moreover, in attempting to restore the bureaucracy's purity of mission, the reform efforts of the late nineteenth century stripped the public career service of its duty to risk itself for the qualitative enhancement of the citizenry.

Duty, so perceived, would seem to assume the character of a cause or, if you will, a categorical imperative that, according to Lionel Trilling, could validate the personal life that obeyed it. A categorical duty, thus viewed, creates for the individual an inner imperative which guides the individual with a sense of purposeful direction or cause and creates in the individual a sense of personal coherence and selfhood.[37]

As seen in this context, duty carries an individual far beyond the realm of mere compliance, obedience, or even objective performance. Instead, it suggests an energetic, albeit existential, enthusiasm to experience the purely inner satisfaction, personal affection, or genuine love that is realized when duty provides purposeful direction to a transcendent cause. Nevertheless, duty to a cause that is peremptory and absolute must be infused by an impulse of *caritas* if it is to avoid degenerating into a dutifulness that is mechanistically contrived or situationally expedient. If one is to say, "I thought it my duty to risk myself for you," such duty clearly has to be found in a love for some other human being, or, in a less personalized sense, in a sincere affection or genuine respect for some transcendent cause or sense of purposefulness. Viewed from the perspective of H. Richard Niebuhr, the distinguished American theologian, it is the cause or sense of purposefulness that sustains and feeds the relation, and a community can be a community only by virtue of such a common and binding cause.[38]

Our constitutional democracy rests on the basic notion of the inviolability of human dignity, and the justifications for our governmental system and the public policy process rest solely on the extent to which this categorical imperative of democracy is defended and enhanced. While public officials can legitimately be held accountable to uphold the inviolability of human dignity, it is the public administrators for whom this notion of duty has particular importance, since it is the bureaucrats who stand opposite the citizens on a face-to-face, day-to-day basis as the actual implementation of public policy unfolds. If public administrators are to move beyond the role of boundary guarding agents, engaged solely in the transfer of quantitative goods and things, they must—in the fashion of the early Federalists and early Agriculture Department administrators—become motivated by commitments to a purposeful cause and a sense of duty that transcend the specific situational circumstance and extend beyond to the categorical imperative of democracy itself—that is, the enhancement of the quality of life of the individual citizen.

In this context, one is reminded of a comment by George Eliot, the British author, as reported by Lionel Trilling. "God, she said, was inconceivable. Immortality was unbelievable. But it was beyond question that Duty was 'peremptory and absolute.'"[39] In a strikingly similar fashion, the American philosopher Josiah Royce noted that we cannot live without a cause, without some object of devotion, some center of worth, something on which we rely for meaning.[40]

The notion of duty as a love or an intense inner commitment to a cause that extends beyond the exigencies of the moment should constitute a specific attribute of the public administrator as agent of the citizen. Lionel Trilling, in commenting on the work of Jane Austen, provides an interesting insight that can be relevant in this regard. Austen, he notes,

> was committed to the ideal of "intelligent love," according to which the deepest and truest relationship that can exist between human beings is pedagogic. This relationship consists in the giving and receiving of knowledge about right conduct, in the formulation of one's character by another, the acceptance of another's guidance in one's own growth.[41]

Trilling is correct in noting that life perceived as an aspect of instruction is scarcely a new vision. Nonetheless, the relevance of his observation in regard to our current predicament seems especially pertinent, particularly at a time when rapidly accelerating social complexity makes right conduct highly problematical. Certainly, insofar as the effective implementation of public policy is concerned, it is the federal bureaucracy that enjoys the most advantageous position vis-à-vis the citizenry to inform and to be informed, to guide and to be guided. The cause that binds the citizens and the public administrators in our constitutional system is a shared respect or love for the democratic ideal of intrinsic individual goodness. The attainment of this ideal is directly related to the "intelligent love," the pedagogical love that potentially exists between the citizenry and the bureaucracy. It is this binding force that makes interpersonal trust possible, and it moves democracy beyond the banalities of a mechanistically contrived constitutionalism to the transcendent position of a dynamic, holistic process guided by a "living," organic spirit.

To be sure, for those who tend to perceive public-sector career bureaucrats as ominous, murky-gray forces who operate somewhere on the other side of midnight, the argument advanced will surely be discomfiting. Even those who have a more benign view of public administration and administrators may be inclined to echo Glaucon, who, in Plato's *Republic*, says to Socrates that his heavenly city is too ideal and does not exist "anywhere on this earth." Socrates's answer to Glaucon, however, should not be summarily dismissed; it holds particular relevance for administrator and citizen alike if the ideal vision of American democracy is to carry into the twenty-first century. "Glaucon, whether such a [city] exists or ever will exist in fact, is no matter; for he will live after the manner of that city, having nothing to do with any other." But, Socrates adds, "in heaven there is laid up a pattern of it, methinks, which he who desires may behold, and beholding, may set his own house in order."[42]

Crisis and complexity are relative and relational terms. No age has a monopoly on either, and virtually every decade of our history has been infused with both. The enormous expansion of public policy activity by the federal government during most of the twentieth century has imposed an almost intolerable burden on those who bear the responsibility to ensure that the laws are faithfully executed. In the early nineteenth century, the responsibility of political faithfulness was viewed by most public administrators primarily as an absolute duty to strive for the true sense of *caritas* inherent in democracy. Perhaps this can be attributed to the unsophisticated naiveté that infused our political process with a dynamic hopefulness at that time. By the end of the nineteenth century, democracy and the federal bureaucracy were saved from the ravages of the spoils system by the combined energies of the reform movement. Nevertheless, the long-term consequences of this movement that have manifested themselves throughout the second century of our constitutional enterprise have had some serious, debilitating effects. The categorical imperative of the federal bureaucracy has steadily diminished during the twentieth century with the exception of its heightened revival during the crisis years of the Great Depression and the Second World War. The earlier sense of duty seems now, as we attempt to recall it, a nostalgic anachronism. Yet the search for excellence in management circles, public and private, is proceeding in directions that are strikingly reminiscent of a past that may not, in fact, be so distantly removed from our present reality. The qualities of organizational and managerial excellence that are currently being "discovered" or "reinvented" are, in reality, qualities of human interpersonal relationships that are profoundly ethical and moral in character.

The Ethos of Bureaucracy

At the present time, some very exciting and challenging changes are taking place inside public-sector organizations, especially at subnational levels. At the local level, for example, public administrators in numerous communities throughout the nation are operating—perhaps out of the stark necessity for sheer survival—with a very clear and pronounced willingness to risk. As a consequence, in many instances, as the notion of the democratic ideal becomes revived, the notion of citizenship is being reclaimed. The situation that relates the citizenry to its national government, however, is not as bright. There is more than sufficient evidence to indicate that the policy outputs of the federal establishment are still being treated variously by the body politic with boredom, distrust, and/or futility. The constitutional sense of duty at this level of government seems hopelessly

enmeshed in the webwork of a mechanistic constitutionalism of dutifulness. Certainly, as we broach the twenty-first century, there is
little to suggest that the categorical imperative of democracy is given
much more than rhetorical flourish at the national level of government. Are the elements for such an ethic irretrievably lost, or are
they simply lying dormant? The premise advanced here is that they
exist in the ethos of a profession that has survived the centuries; but,
more directly, these elements exist in the ethos of a bureaucracy especially fitted to the contours of our democratic constitutional tradition. Let me attempt to capsulize the essence of this premise as it has
been developed in the preceding chapters.

The prime virtue of our constitutional democracy is derived from
two basic sources. First, it is based on the Greek notion of happiness, as modified by the Old Testament dictum of love of God, and,
second, on the Old Testament covenantal notion of obligation or
duty, as amplified in the New Testament as love of neighbor. These
two themes, happiness and duty, form the keystone of our democratic archway. Happiness, as in Jefferson's "pursuit of happiness,"
is a love—an absolute and unwavering faithfulness—in the divinely
inspired, transcendent goodness of democracy. Integral to this notion of happiness or goodness are the concepts of the absolute sanctity of individual human worth and dignity (life) and of individual
human reason and choice (liberty). Thus, the Constitution of the
United States (and the Bill of Rights) can be viewed as the positive
document designed to ensure, protect, and guarantee the "natural
law" intention of the Declaration of Independence—that is, the inalienable rights of life, liberty, and the pursuit of happiness.

The Constitution, including the Bill of Rights, implicitly embodies
the notion of the transcendent purposefulness and goodness of democracy. Its primary focus, however, is on its explicitly articulated
sense of duty or obligation as, for example, the explicit obligation of
the president to ensure that the laws are *faithfully* executed. If one
integrates the sense of happiness or transcendent purposefulness
with the sense of duty or obligation, it becomes apparent that the
primary function of government is to maintain an environment that
is fully conducive to the qualitative enhancement of the life of the
citizenry. This purposeful function constitutes the categorical imperative of democracy. The proposition advanced in the preceding pages

rests on the assumption that the extent to which this categorical imperative of democracy can be even approximately realized depends on the extent to which individual career public administrators who constitute the bureaucracy can internalize this imperative as their own mandate for the democratic implementation of public policy.

The transcendent goodness of constitutional democracy depends on the manner in which its specific policy goals and objectives are implemented by a cadre of professional managers and administrators. Given a high degree of rational competency, ethical maturity, and a shared vision of the transcendent purposefulness of democracy, the bureaucracy stands as the agency of the citizen; it stands as the primary problem-solving and problem-dissolving policy mechanism in our system; it stands, in the final analysis, as both our first and last line of defense in making democracy "work." Given a low degree of rational competency, ethical maturity, and/or transcendent vision, however, the hopes and visions engendered by the ratification of the Constitution are bound to be dashed on the rocks of parochialism. As discussed in more detail in chapter 6, individual bureaucrats can be infused with a sense of transcendent purposefulness or with a sense of egoistic self-interest generated by a politicized pragmatism. Both value perspectives have been manifested in the course of our constitutional development; but the implications of each perspective, as related to the categorical imperative of democracy, are as different as the vision of light is from the vision of darkness.

To be sure, administration is politics; the bureaucracy is an integral part of our political system; and politics in a democratic context is clearly the art of the possible. We would have it no other way. A commitment to the art and artistry of the possible, however, incurs an inherent tension. On the one hand, a notion of "the possible" can be viewed in terms of a transcendent hopefulness of that which is, is good. On the other hand, "the possible" can be perceived in terms of a pragmatic expediency of that which is good enough, is good enough. Bureaucracy stands as the critical intervening variable in determining the outcome of this complex equation, and in this regard even a high degree of intellectual competency, ethical maturity, and purposeful direction cannot be taken as determinative. This cluster of critical values can be decidedly skewed by a conscious choice between risk-incursive or risk-aversive behavior. Either can be pursued in the name of professional competence, ethical integrity, and purposefulness, but, again, the relational value impact of risk-incursive as opposed to risk-aversive behavior on the categorical imperative of democracy is, itself, fundamentally and categorically different.

Thomas Jefferson certainly sensed the dynamically different import attached to these contradictory attitudes of risk. It was Jefferson's perception of public service that led us through our first dark age. The astute foresight he evidenced at that time seems particularly striking when applied to the notions of public service that prevail today as we attempt to manage and control the vast complexities of our current condition. "I thought it my duty to risk myself for you." This, in itself, captures the total essence of the spirit of public service as revealed in the categorical imperative of our constitutional democracy, as well as the American character. Moreover, the public-service vision of Jefferson can serve very well as a response to the fundamental query advanced by Waldo in his valedictory lecture series: "Why would an instrument [bureaucracy] designed to be impersonal and calculating be expected to be effective in delivering sympathy and compassion?"[43] Clearly, it is apparent that an administrative cadre committed to serve in the spirit of democracy was foremost in the minds of the Federalists, who initially fashioned the "instrument" we cursorily refer to as bureaucracy. Aside from the obvious meaning normally associated with the term "public service," there was a more substantive expectation in the minds of the Founding Fathers that those who implemented the laws of the new Republic would also be the "ministers" of the new secular creed, democracy. This vision of public service is explored in depth in the following chapter.

4
The Spirit of Public Service

Service as the Center of Value

The notion of service is clearly evidenced throughout the history of human civilizations. From the earliest of ancient Chinese empires and Egyptian dynasties to the Roman empires, and throughout the Middle Ages to the present day, the idea of committing oneself to a life of service (as opposed to being impressed into duty) is reflected with such frequency as to become commonplace. Yet, the notion of service is anything but a "common" phenomenon.

In fact, the demands associated with a commitment to serve some "higher authority"—however that term may be defined historically—can constitute one of the heaviest burdens that any individual can assume in the scheme of human behavior. Indeed, such demands generally include a universally recognized set of prerequisites such as willing subordination, loyalty, trustworthiness, and an optimistic—that is, hopeful—vision of the future as represented by the "higher authority," however defined.

Biblical, ancient, and medieval history record numerous examples of what we would refer to today as "civil" service—service in the company of an emperor, pharaoh, king, or pope. The titles of those individuals who served in this capacity may sound obscure, quaint, or prosaic to our contemporary ears—tax farmer, cuptaster, guardian of the funerary roles, estate agent, controller of the wardrobe, and mastersmith of the Forest of Dean.* Nonetheless, the or-

---

* Tax farmer: the royal governments of ancient Egypt solicited bids from wealthy citizens interested in serving as contract tax collectors in Egypt's territorial possessions, with contracts usually let to the highest bidder.

Cuptaster: in the ancient world, the individual who stood closest to the king or emperor and who enjoyed the monarch's complete confidence; de-

ganizational, psychological, and existential demands—obedience, loyalty, trustworthiness, and optimistic courage—imposed on the individuals who held these positions are no less meaningful today.

Closely associated with the notion of service is the notion of duty, and the earliest of biblical history informs us that many of the demands of duty imposed on Yahweh's servants and the servants of His people are directly relevant to our own contemporary situations. For example, Jethro explained to Moses[1] the principle of the division of labor in a manner that would make Max Weber proud. The prophets, particularly the bumbling Jonah and the dedicated Jeremiah, revealed human traits that still ring true today. Jonah, for instance, seems strikingly modern—first, in his determination to avoid implementing an unpleasant assignment, and, second, in expressing his frustration and anger when, having carried out the assignment to the letter, the action was rescinded by the same superior who initiated the order. Jeremiah labored indefatigably as a dedicated and loyal change agent to reverse the spreading apostatizing behavior that was destroying the soul of the people of Israel, only to see his mission of service end in total and unmitigated failure. And, of

---

spite the menial connotation, the cuptaster usually held the status of being the monarch's chief of staff.

Guardian of the funerary roles: royal official in Egyptian dynasties responsible for the funeral arrangements of the king, princes, and other noble family members.

Estate agent: specialists in medieval England who managed the widely scattered estates of the great lords and who were given the overall responsibility for total land-use management, the primary objective being to create a surplus of resources.

Controller of the wardrobe: chief administrator of the king's household staff in medieval England; the wardrobe served as the entry-level organization for bright young men to learn the intricacies of the Royal Court and to become skilled in secretarial work, finance, diplomacy, and logistics.

Mastersmith of the Forest of Dean: the Forest of Dean was, in fact, the "royal arsenal" of thirteenth-century England; placed under the supervision of a master blacksmith, it was his responsibility to provide not only such building materials as nails, hammers, and picks to meet the requisitions of the king's building projects but also all manner of weapons (and horseshoes) to equip the king's military forces.

course (but not incidentally), there were the watchmen who were the sentinels of the day and the night, and who formed the defense system of that time. It was the watchman on whom the people depended to ensure their safety and well-being. His duty was to spot the enemy and warn the people. He could see the danger. They could not. If the watchman did his duty, no enemy crept up unnoticed. If he failed in his duty, he was guilty of great harm to his people.

Viewed even from a negative perspective, there were characteristics emanating from the service cadres of the early biblical period that are certainly not unfamiliar to the modern impulses of public service. There were false prophets who were not ashamed of their committed abominations ("they did not know how to blush"), and irresponsible watchmen ("His watchmen are blind, they are all without knowledge; they are all dumb dogs, they cannot bark; dreaming, lying down, loving to slumber"). Of course, the notion of service or duty need not be anchored to a religious base. Again, history is replete with examples of a "civil" service that was devoid of any formal religious sectarian or denominational perspective. The oath taken by all who were selected to serve in the governance of Athens, the cradle of democracy, is a good example.

> We will strive for the ideals and sacred things of the city, both alone and with many; we will unceasingly seek to quicken the sense of public duty; we will revere and obey the city's laws; we will transmit to this city not only not less, but greater, better, and more beautiful than it transmitted to us.[2]

One can also consult the histories of thirteenth-century England and read that

> it should be said that all personnel of the Edwardian household, particularly those of the wardrobe, were loyal and devoted servants, ever mindful that Edward I was master and that to him they owed their position and advancement.... Chancellors like Robert Burnell and John Langton came to their positions only after long and faithful service in the wardrobe and the chancery. The wardrobe was the school of the typical Edwardian official; it was a school dominated by one master, Edward, who observed

the performance and talent of his servants and appointed them to key positions in his government. Almost without exception, these officials were interested in their professional tasks; they left politics and high intrigue to the great magnates.[3]

As noted previously, George Eliot could speak of God as inconceivable, immortality as unbelievable, but Duty as peremptory and absolute. If, however, duty is viewed as a categorical imperative, it is only reasonable to ask, duty to what or to whom? Those of an older generation are certain to recall the nefarious example of duty in the Third Reich, or, more recently, duty in the service of Saddam Hussein.

The notion of duty as an end in itself, as unquestioned allegiance to some "higher authority," or as a categorical imperative of the first order, is not only vacuous but dangerous. Thus, H. Richard Niebuhr can, at first glance, appear to be in agreement with George Eliot when he says, "to deny the reality of a supernatural being called God is one thing; to live without confidence in some center of value and without loyalty to a cause is another."[4] Niebuhr, however, then proceeds to develop this theme of the center of value in a manner that seems strikingly appropriate for a life lived in the service of democracy. As seen by Niebuhr, the individual who has confidence in a center of value and is loyal to a cause

> is related to an actuality that transcends his own, that continues to be though he ceases to exist. He is dependent on it as it is not dependent on him. And this applies even more to his significance than to his existence. The community is not so much his great good as the source and center of all that is good, including his own value. But the society is also his cause; its continuation, power, and glory are the unifying end in all his actions. The standard by which he judges himself and his deeds, his companions and their actions, by which also he knows himself to be judged, is the standard of loyalty to the community.[5]

Examples of service in this mode are certainly not rare in the annals of history, and they are characterized by a center of value and a system of belief that incorporate, yet transcend, the impulses of obedience, loyalty, trustworthiness, and courage generated in the service of some secular authority. Such values and beliefs include a faith in some transcendent good, a hope in the future realization of such a good, and an absolute love for the good, as well as a willingness to share it with others—any other. Our perception of a democratic "public" service, as we think of the term today, may not accord with this mode of service, but, undeniably, history is replete with examples of individuals who were moved to serve their neighbors, as well as strangers, solely on the basis of a faith, a hope, and—as even Machiavelli certainly would concede—a firmness tempered by charity.

For example, we learn from the Book of Genesis that Joseph, son of Jacob, became (after he was "done-in" by his eleven jealous and resentful brothers) the chief administrative officer of Egypt.[6] His dedication to his duty in the service of the Pharaoh was exceeded only by his superior competence. And yet, when confronted with his long-lost brothers (who represented the future tribes of Israel, i.e., "the people"), Joseph shifted from his role as a dutiful servant of the Pharaoh and was motivated by the most humanistic impulses of faith, hope, and love as reflected in the *Shema*.* As one scholar has written,

> The story of Joseph ... shows us this picture of man in wonderful perfection. In scene after scene it depicts a young man who through discipline, modesty, knowledge, self-mastery ... had given a noble form to his whole being, and who in weal or woe always remains the same. Before Pharaoh he proves himself a shrewd counsellor, and before his brothers the man who can be silent, who represses his natural emotions, and finally the one who "covered up all sins with love."[7]

The story of Joseph had a "happy" ending, but the formula of faith, hope, and love is no guarantee for success. Consider, once

---

* *Shema* ("hear"): The inspired *Shema* prayer is the basic expression of faith recited daily by all Jews. "Hear, O Israel: The Lord our God is one Lord; and you shall love the Lord your God with all your heart, and with all your soul, and with all your might." Deuteronomy 6:4–5 (RSV).

again, Jeremiah, who labored dutifully with a single-minded sense of mission for forty-five years among the people of Israel to implant a center of value and a system of belief, both structured around the notions of faith, hope, and love, only to be recorded in history as a "servant" who failed. Jeremiah alienated the "local" government officials who "wanted to convict him of high treason for undermining government policy."[8] What modern-day public administrator cannot identify with the plight of Jeremiah when it is recorded that "the kings and their officials were most disturbed [with Jeremiah] because other [false] prophets spoke words of encouragement and support" for their policies?[9]

Jeremiah's faith, hope, and love for the people knew no bounds. Nevertheless, the kings "won"; their public policies allowed the people to prosper in a utilitarian sense. Jeremiah was forced into exile at the end of his life, and the Israelites continued to "burn incense to the queen of heaven and pour out libations to her"—they "saw no evil."[10]

Also, consider the situation that existed as a result of the Black Death that swept across the European continent in the fourteenth century. As Marvin Becker and Daniel Lesnick explain in their respective studies,[11] the health and social welfare problems that confronted Florence were of monumental proportions. As a result, the manner in which the Florentine government of the day responded to the crisis revealed an attitude of civic responsibility that gradually shifted from a narrow concept of duty to an expansive and elevated sense of self-actualized responsiveness and responsibility on the part of the total community for the care of its underprivileged neighbors.

Quantitatively elaborate and qualitatively superior health, welfare, and human services systems gradually took shape in a context in which the government, in conjunction with other community organizations, assumed direct responsibility for the care of the indigent, infirmed, aged, orphaned, starving, dying, and dead. The net result was (1) a dramatic increase in the democratization of Florentine government and public participation in the policy process, (2) a rising ethical-moral consciousness among the body politic, in general, and (3) a deeply felt sense of civic obligation that was driven by a sense of moral good, rather than a legislatively mandated legal obligation.[12]

For the Florentines, no distinction existed between their role in civic life and the ethos of *caritas*. "Appreciation of the associated life was rooted in his [the citizen's] ample definition of charity.... He proclaimed the primacy of faith, existentially understood, as well as the overarching need for *caritas* if the human community was to flourish."[13] Elsewhere Becker notes, "Philanthropy was ... converted into a way of life rather than a series of isolated gestures. Charity lost much of its dramatic and episodic character as it was trans-valued into a systematized sequence of interrelated acts."[14] In the same context, Becker adds,

> Efforts were made to authenticate new social values and formu-late codes of behavior more relevant for individuals living in greater isolation. To modern scholars, the stress on charity and love might indeed look evasive until one realizes that they sur-faced with compelling force. These virtues alone could foster the family, guard the city, and even enlarge a Florentine empire.... Man's dignity did not reside in solitary experience or in strategic personal relationships. Neither pride of caste nor cultivation of autonomous feelings of selfhood were sufficient to endorse this *dignitas*; instead, man's consciousness of his solidarity with all men was quintessential.[15]

Unfortunately, candor compels us to recognize that the values of Florentine faith, hope, and *caritas* were soon replaced by a new so-cial tone and temper focusing on individual self-interests and compe-tition, perhaps best exemplified by the writings of Machiavelli. Nev-ertheless, we can be confident of the objective facts of the situation. That is to say, at a certain point in the history of Western civiliza-tion, a community came together to serve each other on the basis of the existential impulses of *caritas*, rather than on the basis of the logic of utility. The net result was that the attitudes of the Florentine society of the time "contributed to a belief in an organic, noncom-petitive society in which man subordinated egoistic impulses to *il bene commune*"—the good society.[16] In passing, one can only high-light the quotation from the German philosopher Friedrich Nie-tzsche that Becker uses to introduce his excellent article: "In the long run, utility is simply a figment of our imagination and may well be the fatal stupidity by which we shall one day perish."[17]

Foundational Virtues

To be sure, the notions of faith, hope, and love are not, at least by contemporary standards, generally recognized as significant components of public administration in America today. Instead, it is the logic of utility that still provides the basic rationale for the classical management tenets of efficiency and control. Nevertheless, if public service is to be viewed as an integral component of our democratic political system, Nietzsche's observation concerning the logic of utility has to be taken seriously. In this regard, few management tenets today can improve on the intuitive administrative dictum suggested to Moses by his father-in-law, Jethro,[18] and more recently elaborated and refined by Martin Landau and Russell Stout Jr.: to manage is *not* to control.[19] That is to say, to manage is to develop—creatively, heuristically, prudently, efficiently, and effectively (i.e., entrepreneurially)—the human and organizational resources available to deal with the multiple ambiguities associated with turbulent complexity in the organization's external environment. As noted in chapter 1, repeated efforts to instill this entrepreneurial spirit have been attempted throughout much of the twentieth century. Since the 1960s, efforts to amplify and refine the strategies, tactics, and techniques of advanced management methods have progressed at a seemingly exponential rate and, as a consequence, several generations of students educated in this mode have infused the ranks of executive branch bureaucracies. To paraphrase political scientist Richard Neustadt's[20] comment concerning the American presidency, the public bureaucracy is no place for amateurs.

As the twenty-first century begins, public-sector managers must be specialists by training and application, and professionals by temperament and commitment. Viewed in the dispassionate and detached light of rational objectivity, it is the professional bureaucrats who are expected to provide leadership, demonstrate competence, and reveal confidence in their abilities to maneuver successfully through the complex managerial decision-making maze of contemporary policy systems. Over the course of the past decade, however, public-sector managers in the democratic political systems of the United States, Western Europe, and, most recently, Eastern Europe, as well as the republics of the former Soviet Union have been forced to confront a public-sector reality different from that supported by either the logic of utility or the logic of entrepreneurship. That is to say, a different center of value has emerged in the form of an explicit and persistent public demand for a sense of ethical consciousness to be reflected in the managerial decisions made by those who serve in the name of democracy.

This is not to suggest that the current emphasis on the development of codes of ethical mandates has resulted in the displacement of the conventional canons of professionalism. On the contrary—and especially in connection with the implementation of public policy—the basic canons of bureaucratic management must now be viewed in juxtaposition with the core values of public-sector ethics. Furthermore, to suggest that the linkages that have been attempted between these two sets have been effected smoothly and effortlessly is to view the current state of professional ethics in its most superficial, if not artificial, context.

In far too many instances, the current attention assigned to ethics in bureaucratic circles can be viewed as a supplement to the organizational manuals of standard operating procedures. In the United States, at least, workshops, seminars, and conferences on political and administrative ethics currently abound in such variety that it is virtually impossible to keep abreast of the oncoming tide. From procurement to accounting to budgeting to personnel ad infinitum, "ethical" maxims come at the professional managers from all directions. The business of ethical consultants now constitutes one of the fastest growing cottage industries in the United States.

Unfortunately, the net result of this rather furious effort has been less than impressive. Public-sector executives and policy managers are fast becoming victims of information overload. At worst, the dos and don'ts of procedural ethics can very quickly compound into a supersaturated solution of obscure ambiguity. At best, the tour guides of ethics have become expert in guiding their audiences through the barrier reefs of "what *can* I do?" but they remain totally "in-expert," if not woefully inept, in resolving the perennial question, What *should* I do? The situation that has resulted, to recall a passage from Paul Ricoeur, is that we seemingly have become superbly adept in effecting "a ritualization of the moral life and a moralization of ritual."[21]

Professional career administrators in the public sector today are, above all else, keenly attuned to the craft of political pragmatism and are, in most instances, loath to acknowledge the intrinsic and purposeful benefits to be gained by incorporating the value of a moralistic ethics into the daily operating procedures of their respective enterprises. Both in theory and in practice, public administrators frequently find it convenient to gloss over the historical traditions of ethical-moral values in American democracy. Many of these same individuals, however, are the first to subscribe to the seemingly infinite diversity of instructional methods designed to "teach" administrative and policy officials how to shape their organizations into ethical "centers of excellence." One can dismiss many of these methods as overly simplistic, but three generalizations about modern management approaches to such ambiguous and often vacuous notions as quality and excellence can be advanced.

First, despite the plethora of current managerial "laundry lists" designed to enhance productivity, job satisfaction, and the quality of life of the body politic, the similarities of these lists are far more striking than their differences. That is to say, regardless of the "spin" that can be placed on the various pursuits of excellence such as total quality management or reinventing government, the notion of service to some end other than the self reigns paramount. The team may come first, or the organization may come first, or even "the people" may come first. Seldom, however, is the notion advanced that for public servants, the ethical-moral values inherent in democracy must come first.

The second generalization is a logical extension of the first. Namely, although most of these prescriptions tend to reveal a basic set of management values, another set of values—which can only be described as ethical-moral in nature—is implicitly (if not unconsciously) encased in the core of the "quality/excellence" reinvention clusters. For example, one persistent theme is a clear emphasis on imaginative, innovative, and creative thinking. This emphasis, however, provides virtually no recognition of the fact that such types of thinking and acting carry with them significant ethical-moral impulses. As the American theologian Stanley Hauerwas notes,

> "Imagination" and "the moral life" ... are not two separate subjects which must be brought into relation; rather, they are but two aspects of the same reality. For "imaginative" persons cannot be such without some virtues, and "moral" persons cannot be so without those virtues which compel us to be "imaginative."[22]

And third, as a consequence of the second generalization, examples of "quality" performance or operational "excellence" inevitably focus on managers who heuristically (and, again, often unconsciously) devise their own innovative and imaginative formulas for success that reflect, intuitively and frequently quite fortuitously, an ethical-moral sense of consciousness.

Particularly when applied to the public sector, the fact that such examples of quality and/or excellent performance can only be viewed in idiosyncratic terms leads to a disturbing conclusion: namely, public administration, as a profession, is either unable or unwilling to acknowledge explicitly the critical importance and relevance of the core ethical-moral values that are intrinsic components of the spirit of democracy. These intrinsic ethical-moral values form the dynamic impulses of public service and need to be considered much more seriously than they have been in the past. This is especially true in connection with three foundational virtues that form the core of democratic public service.

Loyalty, for example, is considered a fundamental element of any viable organizational system, public or private. It is inevitably cited as the basic organizational bond that fuses a diverse group of human beings into a meaningful whole. By the same token, loyalty must be viewed as a reciprocal relationship; in fact, it is multidimensional —it must flow in all directions and relate all individuals in the organization to each other. On the other hand, loyalty is just one side of the organizational effectiveness coin; the other side is trust. Thus, loyalty and trust are integrally related—"I learn to trust in response to evidence of loyalty; I learn to be loyal in response to revelations of trustworthiness."[23] Both trust and loyalty are relational concepts and their essence depends on reciprocal response. In fact, whether it is apparent or not, loyalty and trust form the twin energizers of what is generally referred to in biblical history as faith. The truth of the matter is that ethics is, in part, derived from faith—from loyalty and trust—and the sooner this fact is recognized in the democratic bureaucracies of the world, the more effective their approach to public-sector ethics will become.

The immediate response to this assertion is predictable: "That sounds fine, but faith in what? Whose faith?" To be sure, it is impossible to ignore the historical truth that faith, like duty, if left to its own devices (e.g., "blind faith") has led even democratic political systems and policy organizations to the pitfalls of doom. To paraphrase Reinhold Niebuhr, any faith that is only faith soon degenerates into something less than faith. It must be saved by something more than faith.[24] But what constitutes "more than"? It is this question that leads to a consideration of the second foundational virtue that forms the core of democratic public service.

No organization can survive without plans. Policy planning does not take place in a vacuum or without an optimistic sense of vision that can be translated into a meaningful and purposeful sense of direction. The complex world of democratic pluralism and public policy decision making is, to be sure, driven by a diverse set of atomistic purposes, but to what extent does a policy organization reflect a visionary sense of purposeful direction that provides every member of the organization with an optimistic and holistic response to the fundamental questions "Who am I?" and "What can I hope for?" If the reverse side of loyalty is trust, the reverse side of faith is hope.

Not many public-sector administrators or managers like to talk about hope; it is too soft, too indecisive, too ambiguous. Instead, they are trained to think of planning in terms of a key function that involves a much more precise, objective, and tangible output. Hopes are what dreams are made of, and if, as suggested above, the public policy process today is no place for amateurs, it is certainly no place for dreamers. Yet the relationship between hope and planning cannot be denied. Plans are derived from optimistic visions of the future. To the extent that public-sector managers can fix their faith in the belief that the future is the only hope to improve the present, then planning becomes an ethical and moral imperative of the first order—which is to say, ethics is also derived from hope. Thus, what one hopes for and the faith one invests in that hope will, to a great extent, determine the nature of that individual's sense of ethics—to a great extent, that is, but not completely. There is a third foundational virtue that must be perceived if an authentic sense of service in the spirit of democracy is to be realized.

In order to confront the challenges of democracy with a truly mature sense of ethical consciousness, the democratic bureaucracies of the world—as they close the door on the twentieth century—need to reflect on the insights derived from the unlikely source of St. Augustine, who reminds any who would listen that even Satan could have faith and hope, but he could not love.[25]

This is not to say that democratic political systems have been remiss over the past 100 years in engendering values that can be considered love related, if love is defined solely in terms of congenial accommodation and civility, nationalistic unity, or the sort of ambiguous value inherent in the dictum "The team comes first." Examples of such misplaced notions of love abound and can perhaps best be personified in the pages of fiction that all too frequently reflect the reality of fact. For example, the British author of spy novels John le Carré, in *The Honourable Schoolboy,* has George Smiley, public servant par excellence, advising his colleagues "to be inhuman in the defence of our humanity, harsh in defence of compassion, and singleminded in defence of our disparity."[26] Indeed, if considered only in terms of the internal organizational context of bureaucratic behavior, private-sector corporations and many democratic governments throughout the world have, during the course of this century, invested a "king's ransom" in attempting to design and develop what Abraham Maslow, the distinguished humanistic psychologist, referred to as the ideal eupschyian community—a community in which hundreds, if not thousands, of individuals could be melded into a unified, self-actualized system of optimal social effectiveness.* One cannot ignore the fact that from the early decades of the twentieth century, the administrative systems of numerous public- and

---

* Abraham Maslow, *Eupschian Management* (Homewood, Ill.: Richard D. Irwin, 1965). As used by Maslow, the term *eupschyia* is intended to convey the real possibility open to any collective group of individuals to follow a dynamic pathway toward an ideal state of psychological health, that is,

private-sector organizations have served as the testing ground for organizational psychologists of virtually all stripes in search of the virtues and values that could ensure the presence of an ideal bureaucratic model. In regard to the love ethic, however, one can only conclude that the search has been woefully misdirected.

To be sure, much of the scientific research and development conducted by generations of organizational psychologists has been rooted in a deep substratum of ethical values. Moreover, a valid argument can be made that the twentieth-century search for an ideal set of operative managerial values has consistently evidenced a conscious awareness of the psychological and, indeed, the existential factors that relate to the quality of life and that yield responsible, mature, dedicated, and productive political executives or policy managers. Nevertheless, the differences that set this approach apart from an authentic focus on public-service ethics are far more significant than their similarities.

Love is a many splintered thing and twentieth-century world society seems particularly adept at focusing on its secondary characteristics while ignoring its primary thrust—and maybe for good reason. The true direction of *caritas*, or love, if applied seriously, inevitably moves on a collision course with many of the basic canons of public-sector management. The concept of formal, institutionalized, bureaucratic authority; the notion of detached, dispassionate, objective neutrality; and the almost absolute emphasis placed on rational, routinized, programmed behavior do not form an organizational atmosphere that is congenial to the spread of a love ethic. Viewed from the perspective of most complex organizations, love is a virtue that bureaucracy can ill afford; its potential for the subversion of authority is too well documented; to talk about a detached, dispassionate, objective love is a contradiction in terms; and certainly it is a force that shows no respect for programmed, routinized—that is, habituated—responses.

In the pragmatic context of the democratic political community, the seasoned professional can come to grips with the notion of love

---

the absolute realization of complete and thorough self-actualized behavior on the part of every member of the group. Its stress is on the notion of possibility and not certainty or inevitability.

if it is defined in terms of friendship (*philia*) or happiness (*eudaemia*). If and when it begins, however, to manifest itself in its pure form of *agape*—the complete, total, spontaneous, unsolicited, and unilateral giving of oneself to another with no thought of reward or punishment—it begins to cause serious concern in the ranks of public administration and management, in general. The dreary, if not grim, conclusion to be drawn from this proposition should be apparent: The twenty-first century needs public policy executives and administrators who are true professionals—amateurs, dreamers, and lovers need not apply.

Love and Power

Malcolm Muggeridge, the British journalist and social critic, once disclosed his "lesson of life"—namely, that every person and community (and organization) has to make, in some wrenching, basic way, a decision about whether they are going to behave according to the norms of power or the norms of love. He said you cannot do both. The fact is, however, that the three foundational virtues that are capable of energizing an ethics in the service of democracy cannot dispense with either organization or power. As Mary Parker Follett, the first American woman to establish her credentials as a major organizational theorist and management consultant, noted years ago, power *is* an indispensable and inevitable aspect of democratic life, but only to the extent that it is defined in terms of power *with* rather than power *over*.[27]

To be sure, the manner in which any public-sector organization defines the purposefulness of its power as directed to both its internal and external environments will determine its attitude toward the love ethic, and in this connection it is imperative to recall the previously cited Landau and Stout maxim, "to manage is *not* to control." This is not to say that the love ethic, itself, is not a dramatic manifestation of power. It generates the type of power St. Augustine refers to when he notes that "true prudence is to help those weaker than ourselves in matters in which we are more powerful, if we wish to be aided by someone more powerful than ourselves."[28]

For this reason, one should not be too quick to dismiss the love ethic as a soft, sentimental exercise in self-indulgence. It involves an intense inner discipline and demands a degree of moral toughness that can be found only in ethically mature individuals and organizations. Indeed, it involves a most sophisticated understanding of the use of power as a means to energize the full force of ethical values.

As seen by H. Richard Niebuhr, value is present *whenever* one individual with capabilities and potentialities confronts another individual who limits and constrains, or complements and enhances the intrinsic resources of the other.[29] If viewed in terms of bureaucratic power, the similarity is obvious. It becomes a question of whether a public-sector manager or administrator is willing to share power with, or even transfer power to, a subordinate or a clientele group to enable the subordinate or the clients to grow as mature human beings; or whether the manager will jealously guard his or her power over the subordinate and the clients in a manner designed to maximize a relationship of controlled dependence.

The political theorist Michael Walzer notes in his book, *Exodus and Revolution*,[30] that Moses was neither king nor prince but a simple sheepherder whose reluctance to respond to the call of service was exceeded only by his unwavering faithfulness when he finally did agree to assume the power of leadership. In the hands of Moses, power was used as an energizer of love to guide, to guard, to manage, and, most importantly, to inspire the people with a recognition of their invaluable resources of freedom, equality, and justice. His power was never used to control, to dominate, to oppress, or to deceive. The style of his management of power reflected a mature understanding of the love ethic. Such ethical maturity requires unfaltering confidence in openness to the other—any other—and faithfulness to the human dynamics of reciprocal trust and loyalty. To a very real extent, this Mosaic paradigm of the ethical management of power is directly relevant for our own contemporary pilgrimage.

Long before Walzer, St. Augustine was grappling with the same issue of power. If Augustine's notion of "household" in the following quote can be viewed in the sense of a broader community, the contemporary relevance of the Mosaic paradigm of the management of power should become apparent.

> To begin with, a man has a responsibility for his own household ... [such that] the Apostle [Paul] says, "Anyone who does not

take care of his own people, especially those in his own household is worse than an unbeliever—he is a renegade." This is where domestic peace starts, the ordered harmony about giving and obeying orders among those who live in the same household. ... In the household of the just man who "lives on the basis of faith" ... those who give orders are the servants of those they appear to command. For they do not give orders because of a lust for domination but from a dutiful concern for the interest of others; not with pride in taking precedence over others, but with compassion in taking care of others.[31]

Conflict and challenges to a power utilized in the service of the love ethic are bound to be encountered in the spheres of our contemporary "wilderness." The management of conflict is the primary cost of undertaking the journey. If the costs appear too high, however, public administrators may opt for alternative power paradigms that appear more economical in terms of time and energy. They can follow the lead of others and do what everyone else is doing, which is conformism; or they can do what others tell them to do, which is authoritarianism. In either case, control and domination prevail, and the promise of democracy becomes a wisp of the past.

Moreover, operating in public-sector organizations, the ability to sublimate ego drives for personal rewards, recognition, power, and status requires strong, mature, and self-confident personalities. Even more significantly, it requires that public administrators develop a clear and mature understanding of the fact that the love ethic serves as the keystone of the human side of democracy. Only to the extent that today's administrative officials and policy managers are able to reflect the inner toughness required of this radical ethic can they begin to recognize the true sense of service that is attached to the mature ethical principles of democracy.

Erosion of Mutual Respect

Leonard White wrote in 1961,

The men who had to organize the state and federal governments from 1780 to 1790 found nothing in the books of their time to

guide them. . . . Fortunately, much of the administrative art is synonymous with common sense, sound judgment, initiative, and
courage—basic virtues that were doubtless as ready at hand then
as now.[32]

"Common sense" has always enjoyed a prominent position among
our garden-variety virtues, and especially for public administrators
who must operate constantly in the Janus-faced world of accountability and responsiveness. The thesis advanced to this point admittedly has been focused primarily on public-sector responsiveness to
the ethical-moral impulses inherent in public service. As noted previously, however, closely related to the notion of service is the concept
of duty. Public administration, at all levels of government, is, indeed,
duty bound to recognize, respect, and implement the statutory mandates incorporated in policy enactments by the legislative branch.
Nevertheless, in response to any given policy situation, an ambiguous, multidirectional tension inevitably results among top-level
elected and appointed executives who can agree as to "what *can* be
done," legislative officials who come to agreement as to "what *will*
be done," and career civil service administrators and managers
whose perceptions reflect "what *should* be done" insofar as the day-
to-day aspects of program implementation are concerned.

As Herbert Simon and Victor Thompson, two of the leading figures in public administration, state in their introduction to the reis-
sue of the classic Simon, Smithburg, and Thompson text:

> The flip side of corruption is legislation against conflict of inter-
> est, which, while evidencing a higher level of moral sensibility,
> undertakes to substitute detailed rules and regulations for com-
> mon sense morality, thus making government service less attrac-
> tive and sometimes economically ruinous for honest civil ser-
> vants.[33]

Similarly, political scientist James Q. Wilson, in his volume *Bureaucracy: What Government Agencies Do and Why They Do It*, argues
that public-sector organizations must recapture the vision of their
missions as opposed simply to reacting to the plethora of legislative

constraints which now render them inert.[34] In reviewing Wilson's book, another public administration scholar, Frank Rourke, observes:

> Such a happy outcome is imaginable only in a political system that operates far differently than the U.S. system does today, where there is widespread uncertainty as to the fate of policy goals even after they have been enacted into law, mainly because partisan politicians in both the White House and the Congress nurture a nervous suspicion that the executive officials administering the law may alter its intent. In a setting of this sort, political actors of every description see control over bureaucracy as essential to control over policy.[35]

To be sure, "common sense" dictates that the administrative branch is legally obligated to observe the legislatively mandated "letter of the law," but the fact of the matter is, given the ever-expanding ethical complexities facing democratic societies today, common sense is of little value and may, in fact, be of no virtue in guiding administrators through the procedural maze of legislative mandates and executive rules and regulations. Suspicion, distrust, sometimes outright disdain do not follow a unidirectional course—that is, from top-level political executives and legislators to the career bureaucrats. At the present time, these attitudes are reciprocal and multidirectional. Indeed, one could argue that, throughout our society and among governments at all levels, these attitudes are pervasive. From all indications, the net result among public-sector administrators today, especially at the state and local levels that have suffered the most severe fiscal and budgetary setbacks, is a rising level of uncaring cynicism—a situation that creates a fertile seedbed for the growth of nihilism.

If service is defined solely in terms of duty, the values of obedience, loyalty, trust, and courage can indeed be indelibly imprinted on the virtues of prudence, fortitude, temperance, and justice, but, as was noted in chapter 2, the net result in far too many historical circumstances has been the manifestation of pretense.

In attempting to maintain the artificial appearance of dutifulness, many public administrators have sought to link their commitment of service to the amoral pretense of detached objectivity, neutral competence, and dispassionate rationality. In this regard, one is reminded of the speech by the Third Knight in the American-born, English author and poet T.S. Eliot's *Murder in the Cathedral*. After he and his cohorts, acting on direction of the king, have assassinated Thomas Becket, the archbishop of Canterbury, the Third Knight turns to the audience and states:

> There is one thing I should like to say.... In what we have done, and whatever you may think of it, we have been perfectly disinterested. We are not getting anything out of this. We have much more to lose than to gain. We are just four plain Englishmen who put our country first.... So, as I said at the beginning, please give us at least the credit for being completely disinterested in this business.[36]

By contrast, at various times in the history of American public administration, career public servants have revealed an indomitable faith in the ethical-moral principles embedded in democracy (e.g., during the Federalist era). Moreover, they have frequently affixed their hopes to the visionary promise of democracy (e.g., during the Progressive era), and, as is discussed in detail in chapter 5, they have, on notable occasions, demonstrated a mature and powerful sense of sympathy and enthusiasm in their collective efforts to enhance the qualitative well-being of the citizenry (e.g., during the New Deal years).[37] It should be apparent, however, that for public administrators in democratic societies, the wisdom borne from faith in the political system, the hope reflected in purposeful policy decisions and program implementation, and the love generated in the willingness to incur risks for the well-being of other human beings are not derived simply from the shallow reservoir of common sense or duty.

With 7,000 years of Judeo-Christian biblical history to draw upon, it should not be surprising that the human attitudes of suspicion, distrust, and cynicism are in constant conflict with the foundational ethical-moral virtues of faith, hope, and love. These virtues are deeply embedded in the philosophical, theological, and ideological literature of the ages, and they are the central elements of any mature ethical framework. One cannot ignore the fact, however, that the threats of human suspicion, distrust, and cynicism do, indeed, erode the principal foundations of service on which democracy rests.

In the Service of Democracy

By Reinhold Niebuhr, we are informed that "practically every moral theory, whether utilitarian or intuitional, insists on the goodness of benevolence, justice, kindness, and unselfishness."[38] Although it can be argued that the ethos of democracy is found in the centripetal fusion of these values with the core virtues of service (faith, hope, and love), the history of public administration in America clearly reveals two simple realities. First, periods of such unity are difficult to attain, but even more difficult to maintain, and, second, when periods of such unity have been attained, the concerted conscience of a faithful, hopeful, and caring cadre of career public servants has been clearly evidenced. Unfortunately, the converse is also true. During periods of no national ethical unity, it is generally inevitable that the career public service is the first to be affected adversely by the external and internal centrifugal forces of suspicion, distrust, and cynicism.

On reflection, one conclusion seems to suggest itself. As our democratic system enters into the twenty-first century, the value tensions inherent in democracy seem to be manifesting themselves in anticipation of a critical encounter. If this is, in fact, the case (and the evidence to support this proposition is persuasive), a heavy burden rests on the career public service to assume the initiative in creating among the body politic new possibilities for igniting the centripetal forces of ethical values and moral virtues that reach their point of convergence in the common good.

To labor in the service of democracy is to recognize that all of us are called, in one way or another, in varying degrees of responsibility, to be watchmen, sentinels, or prophets for others—any others —as well as for one another, in attempting to attain the common good. It is a recognition of the fact that a life in the service of democracy is a life of constant instruction, a relationship that, as Trilling notes, consists in the giving and receiving of knowledge about right conduct in the formation of one person's character by another and in the acceptance of another's guidance in one's own growth.[39] In a word, society is dependent on the career professionals in governments at all levels to lead it to the value vision of the common good. As a first step in this direction, public administrators must be willing to confront the suppressive and debilitating constraints that are currently being imposed on "bureaucracy" from all directions, and to reaffirm the values and virtues inherent in the notion of service that have unified the ethical forces of democracy in the past. Public service in the spirit of democracy demands an unqualified commitment to the common good. Nothing less will do; nothing more is needed.

The notion of the common good has been an underlying theme of several of the previous chapters. At this point, it is appropriate to address this concept directly. In the following chapter, the discussion of the common good is narrowly focused on a specific federal agency that, during the time of the New Deal, attempted to apply it as its guide. The manner in which this agency perceived its mission and was guided by its vision of the common good reveals how the central themes of the previous chapters can be drawn together to form a dynamic, holistic system, fully energized by the ethical-moral dimensions of democracy.

5

A Vision of the Common Good

WHAT CAN be said of an agency of the federal government that became a haven of opportunity for a wide variety of university scholars and their students to translate theory into practice, ideas into programs, and values into action? Of an agency that attracted the attention and became an object of serious study by such eminent social scientists as Edward Banfield, Robert Lynd, Gunnar Myrdal, John Gaus, Charles Hardin, Harold D. Lasswell, Grant McConnell, and others? Of an agency that provided the essence of artistic inspiration and literary expression for such major figures as James Agee, Margaret Bourke-White, Erskine Caldwell, John Ford, Alfred Kazin, Archibald MacLeish, John Steinbeck, and Richard Wright, among others?* Certainly one reasonable assumption is that the agency must have been engaged in something unusual and interesting to at-

---

* Political scientist Edward Banfield conducted a study of the FSA's Casa Grande cooperative resettlement project in Arizona; see his *Government Project* (Glencoe, Ill.: Free Press, 1951). The eminent sociologist Robert Lynd was engaged by Roy Stryker to provide guidelines for RA-FSA staff photographers as to what constituted the classical images of America. The adverse consequences suffered by the RA-FSA in their efforts to pierce the barriers of racial segregation provided a rich source of material for Gunnar Myrdal's classic *An American Dilemma* (New York: Harper and Brothers, 1944). John Gaus, along with Leon Wolcott, examined in detail the role of the RA-FSA in their book, *Public Administration and the United States Department of Agriculture* (Chicago: Public Administration Service, 1940). Charles Hardin's scholarly reputation on agriculture policy followed from his 1943 study of the FSA for a special committee created by Chester Davis, then the director of the National Defense Advisory Commission. In 1939 Secretary of Agriculture Henry Wallace invited the political behaviorist Harold Lasswell to provide program guidelines that would yield greater sensitivity among FSA field officials toward the plight of black farm families. And Grant McConnell, in his book *The Decline of Agrarian*

tract such attention. For those who follow "the great game of politics" with a Machiavellian eye, however, a more subtle and darker corollary could be appended to the former supposition: any government agency that creates such attention is destined to live a life that is, in the words of Thomas Hobbes, solitary, poor, nasty, brutish—and, quite probably, short.

The truth of the matter is that in the case of the Resettlement Administration (RA)—established by Executive Order on 30 April 1935—and its subsequent extension, the Farm Security Administration (FSA)—established by law on 22 July 1937—both of these assumptions proved correct. It was an interesting, if not fascinating, bureaucratic venture in its policy mandate, its composition, and its

---

Democracy (Berkeley: University of California Press, 1953), examined in detail the role of the American Farm Bureau Federation in contributing to the ultimate demise of the FSA.

In addition to these social scientists, the RA-FSA also attracted the attention of numerous literary figures. The novelist James Agee worked with RA-FSA staff photographer Walker Evans to prepare a photodocumentary on Southern poverty entitled *Let Us Now Praise Famous Men* (Boston: Houghton Mifflin, 1941). Similarly, the novelist Erskine Caldwell wrote the text to accompany the images of one of America's most famous documentary photographers, Margaret Bourke-White, in their work entitled *You Have Seen Their Faces* (New York: Viking Press, 1937). One of America's leading black writers during the 1930s and 1940s was Richard Wright, who, working with RA-FSA staff photographer Edwin Rosskam, wrote the text of their major work, *Twelve Million Black Voices: A Folk History of the Negro in the United States* (New York: Viking Press, 1941). The eminent poet Archibald MacLeish put together, in his words, "a collection of photographs illustrated by a poem." Entitled *Land of the Free* (New York: Harcourt, Brace, 1938), it contained thirty-three photographs by Dorothea Lange. Lange and her husband, Paul Taylor, also collaborated to produce a photodocumentary volume entitled *An American Exodus: A Record of Human Erosion* (New York: Reynal and Hitchcock, 1939). The literary historian Alfred Kazin, in his classic *On Native Grounds* (New York: Doubleday Anchor, 1956), indirectly related the RA-FSA programs to the artistic works accomplished under the aegis of the Works Progress Administration. John Steinbeck, author of *The Grapes of Wrath*, and John Ford, director of the movie version of Steinbeck's novel, made extensive use of the RA-FSA photohistorical files in compiling research for their respective works.

mode of operation; by the same token, however, the agency faced much criticism and was, ultimately, short-lived.

The Willingness to Risk

When Franklin D. Roosevelt assumed the presidency in March 1933, a new, positive, proactive, and dynamic energy was infused into the policy machine of the federal government. The impulses of the federal government shifted from passive to active states and from purely reactive to anticipatory modes. That is to say, the federal government discarded its negative, detached, and impersonal roles and adopted radically new attitudes toward the notion of governance. For Roosevelt, the choice was simple: the federal government had to embark on a mission to save the nation, and in the process it had to assume the role of *the* agent of change. The tone and temper of this new direction were clearly announced by Roosevelt in one of his early 1932 campaign speeches:

> The country needs and, unless I mistake its temper, the country demands bold, persistent experimentation.... Take a method and try it: if it fails, admit it frankly and try another. But above all, try something. The millions who are in want will not stand by silently forever while the things to satisfy their needs are within easy reach.[1]

Clearly, Roosevelt's message was a call for action rather than inaction, for decision rather than indecision, for hope rather than despair, for risk rather than caution, and for imaginative new ideas rather than rote reactions. As the British political scientist Harold Laski subsequently noted,

> As soon as the American democracy moved into the epoch of the positive state, it could not afford the luxury of dull government. For it is the inherent implication of dull government that the dynamic of the national life is not profoundly effected by its operation; and it is to the inherent dynamic of the positive state that the operations of government are profoundly important. From

this it follows that the government of a positive state must, if it is to be successful, necessarily be a *thinking government*.[2]

Apropos of Laski's reference to a "thinking government" was the formation by Roosevelt, while still governor of New York, of a group of policy advisers, drawn mainly from Columbia University. Dubbed the "brains trust" by Roosevelt, this group included such well-established scholars as Raymond Moley, Adolf Berle, and, the "youngster" of the group, Rexford Guy Tugwell.

As a young economics professor at Columbia University, Tugwell held intellectual convictions centered on the notion of social unity from which could be derived the human impulses of community, co-ordination, and cooperation. Moreover, it is important to note that this notion of social unity was drawn as much from the Federalist visions of Alexander Hamilton as it was from the agrarian virtues of Thomas Jefferson.[3] According to Sidney Baldwin, who wrote the definitive work on Roosevelt's agricultural policies and programs, Tugwell and his reform-minded New Deal colleagues "approached Jefferson from the social rather than the individual side; and they were closer to Hamilton and the Federalists in their ideas about the uses of power; but they were Jeffersonians at heart."[4]

As Tugwell noted in connection with the New Deal programs he drafted for agriculture policy, "it will pay the farmer, for the first time, to be social-minded, to do something for all instead of for himself alone. We thus succeed ... in harnessing a selfish motive for the social good." He then added, "We can even go further with this; we can make [the farmer] contribute toward a long-run program in this way. We can plan for him and with him."[5] This was Federalist Hamiltonianism at its best; for Tugwell, nothing short of a total reconstruction of the nation's economy would suffice.

Roosevelt—as presidential candidate, president-elect, and, finally, as president—relied extensively on the advice and counsel of his "brains trust." Tugwell, for example, was instrumental in having Henry Wallace appointed secretary of agriculture. Wallace, in turn, and with Roosevelt's enthusiastic concurrence, requested Tugwell to serve as one of his assistant secretaries.

Between the November 1932 election and the March 1933 inauguration, Wallace, Tugwell, and other agriculture advisers prepared

PUBLIC SERVICE AND DEMOCRACY

for the president an agriculture policy "package" that was enacted into law on 12 May 1933. Included in this policy program was the Agriculture Adjustment Act (AAA), which established a national agriculture policy, and the Federal Emergency Relief Act, which established a national relief system.

The primary focus of the AAA was a voluntary allotment plan that was linked to a schedule of parity prices. The act authorized the secretary of agriculture to enter into marketing agreements with farmers who were willing to withdraw land from cultivation in return for guaranteed monetary subsidies provided by the federal government. But this was just the tip of the AAA iceberg. The agency became the federal government's agricultural "holding company." It was a large, complex regional structure that became increasingly fragmented by commodity, procedural, and ideological differences.

"From the very beginning, the AAA was a house divided in which competing interpretations of institutional purpose generated considerable tension."[6] Moreover, the tensions that emerged were multiple. First, there was a fundamental division between the liberal farmers who sought to achieve comprehensive socioeconomic reform and the conservative farmers who desired to stabilize production and income levels in the interests of the well-established farm owners. For the most part, this conflict of interests represented a basic division between large and small landowners. Closely related to this inherent strain was a second tension that divided those who saw farming in Jeffersonian terms—as a way of life and as a means for individual spiritual elevation—as opposed to those who viewed farming solely in materialistic terms and as a means for acquiring financial wealth. Finally, a fundamental division was created between the owners of land and the thousands of tenant farmers and sharecroppers who historically constituted an integral component of the American farm system. For the latter group of individuals, the AAA offered no prospect of hope, and it was this group of Americans—half white, half black—who formed the ranks of the nation's dispossessed and homeless rural poor.

These divisive forces began to form as soon as the AAA was created, and they continued to move on a collision course until they clashed in February 1935. The ensuing showdown between the liberal and conservative factions has been characterized as the "purge

106

of 1935." The net result was that the conservatives solidified their control over the AAA and the hopes of the liberal reformers were effectively squelched.[7]

The AAA purge obviously hit Tugwell the hardest. Determined to resign his position in protest, Tugwell could be convinced only by Roosevelt of the wisdom of British philosopher and mathematician Alfred North Whitehead's assertion that the "clash of doctrines is not a disaster—it is an opportunity."[8] Conversely, Tugwell could find satisfaction in the fact that "at least the crust of custom was now cracked. Old doctrines had been challenged. The doors of government were now open to [people] with bold new ideas."[9] Moreover, it was Tugwell who was able to persuade Roosevelt that effective social reform could not be realized within the existing structures of the Department of Agriculture and that only a new agency, independent of the USDA, could offer any hope to deal with the virulent, systemic economic problems that infected the nation. Thus, as a result of this interaction between Roosevelt and Tugwell, there "emerged one of the distinctive agencies of the New Deal—the Resettlement Administration. Conceived in crisis, born without clear-cut congressional sanction, nurtured by the optimism and humanistic spirit of its leaders,"[10] the Resettlement Administration grew out of the "clash of doctrines" and represented for Tugwell the clear opportunity to institutionalize change.

Loyalty to a Cause

Created by Executive Order 7027 on 30 April 1935, and with Tugwell named as its director, the Resettlement Administration (RA) was a completely independent executive agency with three primary policy goals: (1) to restore landownership through the allocation of low-interest loans to farmers who were burdened with marginal or inadequate land; (2) to restore the productivity of ruined land through soil conservation and rebuilding projects; and (3) to resettle—that is, relocate, rehabilitate, and renew—farm families whose agricultural livelihoods had been destroyed by the depression.[11] In putting forth these goals, Tugwell was accused by many critics of being an idealistic, utopian thinker. Actually, his perspective on the future of American agriculture was quite pragmatic. "The family farm seemed to him as much of a primitive past as the small business. . . . If the family farm or the subsistence homestead had a role, it was at best peripheral, exacting a far higher cost than social value justified."[12] Nevertheless, the critics began to assemble almost immediately after the RA was created, and years later, Tugwell reflected: "we were doomed from the start." The primary defect he found was in the "character which failed. And this was not because the human stock was feeble; it was because the environment was hostile to the development of character."[13]

Although the RA was operating under the mandate of the three broad policy objectives cited above, in actual fact, the new agency became a catchall for a wide diversity of projects, programs, and problems that other executive units wanted to get rid of as neatly as possible.[14] In the summer months of 1935, following the creation of the RA, the pace of organizing the agency to meet its mission was frenetic. One of Tugwell's assistants, a former young Republican stockbroker, Lawrence Hewes Jr., recalled the frenzy of the moment:

> For months we had no regular life; we ate and slept as we could. Office hours were a bedlam of telephones, visitors, hourly crises; evenings and weekends were devoted to accumulated paperwork spewed forth by our infantile field organization. We held fingers in dikes of improvisation against bureaucratic tidal waves. . . . But Tugwell took no pride in conducting a first aid program; our real job was to cure the deeper malady.[15]

It was this "deeper malady" that became Tugwell's overriding concern for the future of the RA. It involved human recovery, rehabilitation, and relocation. Despite the then-prevailing political infatuation with the popular mystique of Jefferson's agrarian ideal, Tugwell considered it a cruel and despairing myth.

> Farm ownership? Yes, some day for some, under the right conditions, at their own choice and with a clear view of its costs and after they have demonstrated their ability to rise. But now, most importantly for many, treatment of disease, better diet for children, a mule, some seed and fertilizer, clothes to lift the shame of going ragged to town, some hope for the future, a friendly hand to help

in every farm and home crisis. . . . If we have no intention of attacking poverty at its source, if we only intend to make owners out of a few of the better tenants, the administration ought not to have credit for helping really forgotten families only for doing what democracies have usually done—helped those who needed help because those who needed it more did not count politically.[16]

Thus, despite the multiplicity of diverse programs that were grafted onto the RA structure, the primary mission of the agency was focused by Tugwell and his advisers on rural rehabilitation, which became synonymous in the RA with the visions of the common good. As Baldwin noted,

As a basis for economic analysis or as a blueprint for public policy, this was an exceedingly ambiguous purpose, but as an expression of social and political aspirations, the idea of rural rehabilitation was deeply humanistic and its goals were the improvement of the human condition.[17]

Tugwell anticipated that his critics would begin to mobilize their forces as soon as the RA was organized, and, indeed, almost before the agency was established, its critics began branding it as "communistic." In an effort to neutralize this negative criticism, he "wasted no time in launching an ambitious public information program designed to propagate the faith of the new agency and its prophet."[18]

Tugwell appointed a noted journalist, John Franklin Carter, as head of his information division. They agreed to divide the information division into five sections: editorial, special publications, radio, documentary film, and photohistorical. The photohistorical section was to employ photographers to (1) establish a historical record; (2) provide documentary photographs of relevant and timely news value; and (3) *produce works of art*.[19] To head the photohistorical section, Tugwell named Roy Stryker, a former graduate assistant and a junior faculty colleague at Columbia University. Stryker was an ideal candidate for the position. Thoroughly committed to and familiar with Tugwell's pedagogical methods, research techniques, and value vision for change, he also had an avid interest in the use of the camera as a documentary device and as a teaching method. When Stryker assumed this mandate in the summer of 1935, it provided him with an exciting opportunity to pursue the "great love of his life"—namely, the use of pictures to illustrate and explain abstract ideas. Moving with methodical deliberation, he organized a group of photographers in such a fashion that the vague, ambiguous, and fuzzy mandate of the entire RA was fundamentally transformed into a coherent and purposeful design. Through the combined efforts of Stryker's section, the programmatic necessity of the resettlement policy was graphically, dramatically, and categorically documented. In this regard, Stryker and his staff served principally as agents of change who spanned the boundary between the agency, Congress, and the public. To a very real extent, it was the photohistorical section of the RA that ultimately was instrumental in shaping a new vision of American society.

The gifted and proficient photographers who became Stryker's missionaries of change were, in their own fashion, dedicated visionaries. None, however, came to the RA with a more clearly defined sense of the common good or with a more sharply focused commitment to effect social change than Dorothea Lange. While the public policy process of the New Deal had a significant impact on the thinking and attitudes of virtually all of the staff members of Stryker's unit, Dorothea Lange's impact on the RA public policy process was singularly significant.*

---

* The other principal photographers who served in the RA and/or the FSA were (1) Arthur Rothstein, who was Stryker's graduate assistant at Columbia University, a skilled technician who became an outstanding photographer; he left the agency in 1940 to join *Look* magazine; (2) Carl Mydans, a 35mm expert who resigned in the summer of 1936 and became a staff photographer for *Life* magazine; (3) Walker Evans, who, along with Lange, was the most distinguished of the agency's staff photographers; he left the agency in the summer of 1937; (4) Ben Shahn, a noted painter, lithographer, and muralist who had worked with the outstanding Mexican artist, Diego Rivera; (5) Paul Carter, who was the brother of John Franklin Carter, Tugwell's information director; possessed of a sound technical command but lacking an artistic sense, Paul Carter was released in 1936; (6) Theodor Jung, who had an excellent artistic instinct but no technical understanding of the equipment; he was released after two months; (7) Rus-

A Vehicle for Service

Dorothea Lange was a photographer by profession, a "bureaucrat" by necessity, a change agent by temperament, and a visionary by instinct. She was a professional photographer who, as a result of circumstance, "found" herself drawn into the vortex of the public policy process during the depression years. Throughout her ten-year period in government (1935–45), she was employed by one state agency, two federal agencies, and three federal departments, during which time, as budgets waxed and waned, she was repeatedly hired, fired, and rehired in a manner that became almost routine. She worked on a full-time basis, a per diem basis, and a "piece rate" (i.e., per negative) basis. Even when she was unemployed, her commitment was so intense that she continued to work on a pro bono basis. In the process, she not only became a documentary photographer, par excellence, but she demonstrated consistently what it means in our democratic rhetoric to serve "as a vehicle for others" —that is, to be a public servant.[20]

Ironically, while Stryker was struggling in the early summer months of 1935 to define the objectives of his photohistorical section and its relationship to the overall goals of the RA, an unexpected bit of information came to his attention. As a result of the Executive Order that established the RA, the California State Emergency Relief Administration (SERA), in which Lange had been originally employed as a "temporary typist," was incorporated into the RA, and

---

sell Lee, who was hired to replace Mydans; he was able to establish excellent interpersonal rapport with his subjects; (8) Marion Post Walcott, a well-bred socialite who, in time, developed her own professional identity as a distinguished photographer; (9) Jack Delano, who was hired to replace Rothstein; along with Russell Lee, Delano worked on the Standard Oil project that Stryker directed when he left the federal service; (10) John Vachon, who joined the agency in 1936 as a file clerk and was subsequently promoted to staff photographer; he left the agency to become a staff photographer for *Look* magazine; (11) John Collier Jr., who joined the agency in 1941 and subsequently became a photoanthropologist; and (12) Gordon Parks, a young black fashion photographer who was hired by the agency in 1941; he, too, subsequently became a distinguished freelance photographer.

Dorothea Lange, 1930s
(*Photograph by Rondal Partridge, © 1997 Rondal Partridge*)

she was shifted to the Information Division of the RA Western regional office as a "field investigator, photographer." In effect, she and Stryker were working for the same Division Chief, John Franklin Carter. It took Stryker several months to formulate the direction he wanted his unit to follow, but in August, Lange received a telegram from Lawrence Hewes Jr., asking if she would be interested in joining Stryker's staff. Lange accepted the offer, and on 1 September 1935, she was officially transferred to Stryker's section, although she remained formally attached to the RA Western regional office located in Berkeley, California.

Artistically, Lange's work while in government service is still universally recognized and acclaimed. From her early experience as a portrait photographer, Lange learned that her special gift was her ability to avoid creating the artificial detachment in which most people are photographically framed and, at the same time, to discern, respect, and project the sanctified solitude of the subject's inner being. As she noted in the latter years of her life: "The human face is

the universal language. The same expressions are readable, under-
standable all over the world. It is the only language I know ... that
is really universal."[21]

Lange's professional achievements in documentary photography
and her active involvement in the public policy process were integrally related. In this regard, her work was always intended to effect
change. "All my life," she said, "I tried very hard ... to make a place
where ... what I did would count,"[22] and, as a consequence, she constantly sought to ensure that the results of her work would have some
kind of lasting, positive impact on the lives of other human beings.

Certainly her intentions to be an agent of change cannot be ques-
tioned; her commitment to the common good was the energetic
force of her life. In assessing her professional career as a "bureaucrat"—as one should be able to assess the career of every public servant—what was the relationship between her intentions and her actions? between words and deeds? faith and works? Indeed, given the
thousands of other public-spirited individuals who enlisted in the
cause of the New Deal, and given the magnitude of the complexity
of the federal government during the depression and World War II
periods, what possible effect could a young, low-ranking, woman
photographer have on the outcome of human lives?

Portrait of a Change Agent

Virtually all of Lange's government work was accomplished during a
continuous series of field trips beginning as soon as she was hired in
February 1935 by the California SERA. Her first assignment was in
Nipomo, located in San Luis Obispo County on the south-central
coast of California. Several hundred migrant families had converged
on Nipomo to obtain field work in picking the early spring pea crop.
Unfortunately, the rains came, destroyed the crop, and left the migrants stranded in the wet and cold days of March without food,
shelter, sanitation, and either the gas or the money to move on.[23]

It was Lange's first exposure to the mass exodus from the Farm
Belt states, and the impact of the scene was indelible:

Their roots were all torn out. The only background they had was
a background of utter poverty. It's very hard to photograph a

proud man against a background like that, because it doesn't show what he's proud about. I had to get my camera to register the things about those people that were more important than how poor they were—their pride, their strength, their spirit.[24]

As the frequency of her field trips increased, so did the frequency of reports to the Rural Rehabilitation Division of the California SERA. By deliberate design, these reports routinely incorporated Lange's most effective photographs. The director of the project, Paul Taylor (who subsequently became Lange's husband), was eager to prepare policy officials in SERA for the major recommendations he intended to submit—the construction of government relocation camps that would accommodate all of the basic subsistence needs of the homeless migrant families.

As a result of the efforts of Taylor and Lange, the first two California camps at Marysville and Arvin were built. This effort, small as it may have been, was not without significance. As Taylor noted subsequently, "There were precedents for state and city public housing, but this housing for migrants turned out to be the first federal public housing in the United States."[25] Moreover, Lange's SERA apprenticeship served her well as an introduction to the public policy process; she discovered just how effective her documentary photographs could be in improving the quality of life for a limited number of human beings.

In the months following Lange's appointment to Stryker's Washington staff, she carried out various RA assignments in the western region. In March 1936, at the conclusion of an extended field trip, Lange fortuitously encountered a situation that would not only substantiate her reputation as an exemplary photographic artist but also establish the RA as a pervasive presence in the New Deal administration.

I was on my way [home] and barely saw a crude sign ... which flashed by at the side of the road, saying PEA PICKERS CAMP. I didn't want to stop, and didn't ... so I drove on and ignored the summons. But, then, accompanied by the rhythmic hum of the windshield wipers, arose an inner argument:

> Dorothea, how about that camp back there? What is
> the situation back there? Are you going back? To turn back
> certainly is not necessary. Haven't you plenty of negatives
> already on this subject? Isn't this just one more of the same?

Having convinced myself for over twenty miles that I could continue on, I did the opposite. Almost without realizing what I was
doing, I made a U-turn on the empty highway. I went back those
twenty miles and turned off the highway at that sign, PEA PICKERS
CAMP.

I was following instinct, not reason; I drove into that wet and
soggy camp and parked my car like a homing pigeon. I saw and
approached the hungry and desperate mother as if drawn by a
magnet. I do not remember how I explained my presence . . . but I
do remember she asked me no questions. I made five exposures,
working closer and closer from the same direction. I did not ask
her name or her history. She told me her age, that she was thirty-
two. She said that they had been living on frozen vegetables from
the surrounding fields, and birds that the children killed. She had
just sold the tires from her car to buy food. There she sat in that
lean-to tent with her children huddled around her, and seemed to
know that my pictures might help her, and so she helped me.
There was sort of an equality about it.[26]

Lange sent copies of the photographs to the city editor of the *San
Francisco News,* who published them immediately. In turn, they
were picked up by the United Press wire service and published na-
tionally. As a result, the federal government dispatched 20,000
pounds of food to California to feed the homeless migrants.[27] As reported by the *News* when the federal government acted on the situation, "Ragged, ill, emaciated by hunger, 2,500 men, women, and
children are rescued after weeks of suffering by the chance visit of a
government photographer to a pea pickers camp in San Luis Obispo
County."[28] The *News* followed with an editorial aimed at the county
and state governments for failing to provide the migrants with the
basic necessities for survival.

In the summer months following Lange's March 1936 photograph of the "Migrant Mother" (see frontispiece, p. ii) another RA staff photographer, Arthur Rothstein, recorded what may be the second-most famous photograph of the Stryker enterprise—"Dust Storm Damage, Cimarron County, Oklahoma." Of course, these images were not needed to convince Tugwell and other top-level administration officials of the scope of the problems facing the nation. But, for Tugwell, at least one aspect of the impending November election campaign was clearly fixed: rural poverty was to be made one of the central policy themes of the Democratic platform and the president's campaign speeches.[29] The effects of this political campaign decision were unambiguously perceived by Stryker in well-defined policy and operational terms. Namely, his photohistorical section had to assume the primary responsibility for convincing the nation that the desolate homelessness reflected in the face of the "Migrant Mother" and the barren emptiness revealed in "Dust Storm Damage" were not mere social aberrations but, rather, the twin peaks of the mountainous problem of rural poverty.

As a result of her field trips, Lange urged Stryker to prepare a photographic selection to accompany a report that was to be submitted by the President's Committee on Farm Tenancy. As she explained to Stryker, the project that she proposed should be "aimed at the place where it counts most, Congress."[30] In addition, Lange knew that the U.S. Senate Labor Committee had requested the Department of Labor to submit a report on migrant labor. Since the RA photography files contained hundreds of her prints on the subject, she implored Stryker to let her prepare a photography supplement for this report also.[31] Stryker approved both requests, and it became her responsibility to select the photographs to be included in the reports, since, as Milton Meltzer, one of Lange's biographers, suggests, "the bulk of the pictures in RA's migrant labor file had been made by her and no one knew the story better."[32]

The cumulative impact of Lange's documentary work is impossible to estimate; but one can draw on comments by her colleagues and professional critics. Of her photograph entitled "Six Tenant Farmers without Farms, Texas, 1937," one critic noted,

Dust Storm Damage, Cimarron County, Oklahoma,
1936 by Arthur Rothstein
(*Courtesy of the Library of Congress*)

if you look at the farmers twice, you will be likely to look at them
more than twice, to go back to them occasionally over the years.
You will get to know them, and also something of the world
which they helped make but which is no longer theirs. It is the
photographer's faith that anything really seen is worth seeing, and
to this faith Dorothea Lange adds her own, that anyone really
known is worth knowing.[33]

Certainly one direct impact of the work by Lange and her colleagues in the RA (and its subsequent reorganization as the Farm Security Administration) was evidenced in the shaping of novelist John
Steinbeck's *The Grapes of Wrath*. Steinbeck studied the RA-FSA
photo file when he began work on his novel, and John Ford, director
of the movie, "sought and found primary source material in Doro-

thea Lange's photographs."[34] One commentator, Pare Lorentz, who was a writer and producer of documentary films for the RA-FSA, wrote in *U.S. Camera 1941*:

> Lange, with her still pictures that have been reproduced in thousands of newspapers, and in magazines and Sunday supplements, and Steinbeck, with two novels, a play, and a motion picture, have done more for these tragic nomads than all the politicians of the country.[35]

Lawrence Hewes Jr. concluded that "Lange's photographs had an extremely powerful effect on those who were unaware of the severity of the dislocation problem in the West." Moreover, according to Meltzer, "Hewes ... became convinced that 'she was about the most important thing in the whole show.'"[36]

When Lange finally completed her work with Stryker and the FSA in January 1940, Meltzer concludes:

> The volume of work she turned out was enormous, its usefulness unquestioned, its quality so superb at times as to earn her rank among the masters of photography. What those years added up to for her, she said, was "the greatest education I could ever have been given by anything or anybody."[37]

As noted in 1973 by photographer, critic, and art curator Van Deren Coke,

> Through her photographs the symptoms of the Depression are clearly set forth and through them we can better understand the tragic events of those times. She made intimate contact with the victims.... Her pictures were effective for they were believed. Nothing about them was contrived or artificial; her warmth was so contagious that her subjects were virtually unaffected by the presence of the camera.... [But, also,] Lange's pictures of the Thirties have endured as important referential documents.... They are readily accessible metaphors that speak of ... [individual] suffering and ... perseverance when faced by a society that no longer has a respected place for a segment of that society.[38]

Despite the fact that Lange's professional accomplishments made her, literally, a legend in her own time, perhaps the most revealing insight to the real character of the person was supplied by Lange herself. Some months after her final departure from the FSA, she wrote to Stryker: "I miss FSA, although I have much work to do. Once an FSA guy, always an FSA guy. You don't easily get over it."*

The Loss of Character

The spirit of the RA-FSA was a reflection of the spirit of Rexford Guy Tugwell, and despite the resignation of Tugwell when the FSA replaced the RA in 1937, the focus of the vision of the FSA and its commitment to social change became, if anything, even more intense. According to Baldwin,

> In no sense was the FSA more clearly and consistently a disturber of the peace than in the realm of ideas and attitudes. Despite its pragmatism and, at the same time, its attempt to fly the banner of agrarian idealism, the agency represented an ideological challenge to the status quo—an invitation to combat. In their official issuances, in their testimony before Congress, in their value statements, in their policy choices, in the pattern of their rewards and penalties, in their appointments of personnel, in their spontaneous behavior, in the inferences that could be drawn from their verbal expressions—in virtually everything they did, the leaders of the FSA revealed an ideological strain. And in propagating that ideology, they were evangelists.[39]

---

* Ibid. One month after her final separation from the FSA in January 1940, Lange became a "photographer-investigator" in the Bureau of Agricultural Economics of the U.S. Department of Agriculture. She subsequently held positions in the War Relocation Authority, where she was assigned the responsibility to document the Japanese relocation program; the Office of War Information; and, finally, the U.S. Department of State, where she documented the 1945 opening of the United Nations in San Francisco. In the midst of this project, poor health forced her from government service, and she spent the remaining twenty years of her life re-engaging with her family and working as a freelance photographer of the world. See esp. Meltzer, *Dorothea Lange*, part V.

In this latter regard, the agency was extraordinarily successful. It was able to generate a public information program in the form of visual images that revealed the many faces of poverty in a manner that has generally been acclaimed as unsurpassed documentary artistry. Unfortunately, in pursuing what can be called its pedagogical function, the agency, of necessity, was guided into (or beguiled by) a passion for public recognition and especially congressional approval. In this regard, its success generated its failure, its victories were the precursors of its defeat, and, from the vantage point of a sixty-year retrospection, its life was gained only in its death.

The agency was labeled utopian because of its stubborn effort to elevate in the citizenry an active and dynamic sense of individual and communal moral awareness and ethical responsibility for the well-being of others. Moreover, it was identified as unrealistic in its "holy grail" search for the end of poverty. Neither criticism, however, is exactly accurate. The agency embarked on an odyssey, to be sure, but an odyssey that was grounded firmly in the moral values and the social, economic, and political realities of the day. Foreseeing the end of the family farm as a result of scientific, technological, mechanical, and managerial advances in agriculture, the agency confronted the existent situation—the massive dislocation of families and the critical need for government sponsored relief, resettlement, and rehabilitation programs—with a hopeful optimism, but also with a well-balanced realism. Perhaps it is accurate to say that Tugwell and his disciples embraced a faith that failed. The fact remains, however, that the energy generated by such faith in the democratic vision is the seedbed for decision as opposed to indecision; for action as opposed to inaction; for purposeful commitment as opposed to *acedia*, or not caring. The RA-FSA experience provided a model that energetically embraced the faith and hope of democracy and willingly accepted all the risks that such a commitment entailed. Some twenty years after his New Deal experience, Tugwell reaffirmed the spirit that motivated the RA-FSA:

My final advice to those who are moved by injustice and human needs, and who think they perceive better possibilities through social organization, is to go ahead. Fail as gloriously as some of your predecessors have. If you do not succeed in bringing about a permanent change, you have at least stirred some slow consciences so that in time they will give support to action. And you will have the satisfaction, which is not to be discounted, of having annoyed a good many miscreants who had it coming to them.[40]

The RA-FSA photohistorical section assembled, in serendipitous fashion, a team of professional photographers whose primary function was simply to document the effects of the depression. In carrying out this function, however, they openly revealed the soul of the nation. The images they created stimulated a wide variety of responses—artistic acclaim, an aroused public consciousness, an embarrassed sense of guilt. Many other individuals, however, had vested interests in maintaining the status quo. For those individuals, the work of the photographic section—which revealed them as, to use John Steinbeck's words, "the greedy bastards they actually were" —was viewed with intense contempt, disdain, and resentment. The one person who was fortuitously drawn into this bureaucratic "morality play"—and ironically the one who probably was most responsible for creating in the public mind the images of human dignity as well as the reflections of guilt—was Dorothea Lange.

The impact that Lange had on the policy process was made possible, however, only because she was able to situate herself in an organizational environment that was willing to engage in imaginative efforts at social change. The synergistic dynamics that indirectly fused Tugwell and Lange to each other were fortuitous, to be sure. Significantly, however, it was the bureaucratic design that allowed the head of an agency and a mere staff photographer to direct their energies to the attainment of a shared vision of the "common good." Under the influence of Tugwell, the RA-FSA established a style of management, a policy focus, *and* a value vision of democracy that, now more than ever, needs to be replicated. We can appreciate the vision of a Tugwell and a Lange from a historical perspective, but can we adopt and adapt their vision of sixty years ago to the public policy problems of our day? For example, what did Tugwell mean when he stated that the Resettlement Administration was doomed from the start "because the environment was hostile to the development of *character*"?[41]

One can only conclude that he was referring to the loss of our *democratic* character—that is, the loss of the basic ethical-moral values that define the essence of democracy as a model of the common good. From top to bottom—from Tugwell to Lange—the RA-FSA undertook a search for the "holy grail" of democracy. They did not find it, nor have we over sixty years later. Can we *hope*, however, that our commitment to the essence of the democratic character—the common good—may infuse us with the same drive that energized the Tugwells and the Langes of a previous generation? If not, the democratic and communal notions of "character," "integrity," "wholeness," and "being" are simply blurred images of a forgotten past.

In reflecting on the experiences of the RA-FSA, it should be apparent that the essence of the common good is infused with a dynamic that is fundamentally moral in nature. Unfortunately, we are frequently loath to acknowledge the moral dimension that permeates our bureaucratic-democratic ethos. Moreover, much of the current attention given to public-sector ethics is devoid of any moral relationship. If administration is law in action, then it seems apparent that ethics is morality in action. From this it would follow that the relationship between democracy and bureaucracy must be linked by a moral impulse.

The public-service commitments to the common good that motivated people like Tugwell, Lange, and many others during the depression and World War II years, clearly stemmed from their perspectives of democracy. As stated in the opening chapter, such a perspective requires, at the least, a conscious and mature awareness of the ethical impulses, political values, transcendent virtues, and moral vision that constitutes the dynamic and holistic essence of democracy. To the extent that these normative dimensions can be guided to a point of convergence, the eschatological essence of the democratic common good can become the defining core of our system of governance. It can provide a meaningful sense of purpose to the system's intentions and actions, its policies and laws, and its processes and procedures. Committing oneself to the common good, however, is easier said than done. To return to one of the central themes advanced in chapter 2, the notion of the common good is a natural incubator, so to speak, for the growth of such social pathogenic organisms as hypocrisy and pretense. Yet the concept of the common good endures, just as the efforts to assimilate the canons of bureaucracy into the impulses, values, virtues, and vision of democracy persist. It is this set of circumstances that is examined in detail in the following chapter.

6

Democracy, Bureaucracy, and the Common Good

IT IS axiomatic to state that any and all political systems, from the most liberally governed commune to the most repressive totalitarian regime, need to be administered and managed; every policy decision is an idle thought until it is implemented. In the United States, elected officials at all levels of government must depend on cadres of civil servants to implement the laws, ordinances, and policies in their respective areas of jurisdiction. Regardless of the intentions of elected chief executives, however laudable they may be, or the wisdom of legislative bodies, however profound it may be, once a policy proposal is enacted into law it must be transformed into action. The responsibility for policy and program implementation must be borne by a diverse array of policy, program, functional, and technical specialists and managers drawn from such professions as accounting, business, law, medicine, engineering, social science, public administration, and so forth. These career public servants are expected to ensure that, in our system of democracy, the laws will be faithfully executed.

The central theme advanced in the previous chapters—that the dynamics of democracy must inhere in the qualitative virtues of the career bureaucracy—is, of course, a proposition that does not stand unchallenged. In reviewing the recent role of public administration, beginning with the decade of the 1950s, one is forced to admit that demonstrable evidence in support of this proposition is woefully weak. Considering the United States as an example of the Western world's commitment to democratic governance, the day-to-day management of its own internal public policy process can hardly be characterized as distinguished. Indeed, candor compels one to admit that, from 1953 to the present, the federal, state, and local governments' managerial and service delivery capacities to deal with such problems as criminal violence, drugs, racism, sexism, aging, health, homelessness, illiteracy, infant mortality, and so forth reveal little evidence of either exceptional operational competence or distinctive qualitative virtuousness.

Indeed, if the present mood in the United States is any gauge, there appears to be a strong current running in favor of an increased reliance on the *private* sector for the implementation of public policy. This attitude seems to reflect an enticing conviction that the private sector, governed as it is by clearly focused managerial strategies dictated by an entrepreneurial spirit is more reliable than a commitment by the public-sector's career bureaucracy to the spirit of democracy. The "bottom-line" argument inherent in this assumption is that the pragmatic, "no-nonsense" rubrics of private-sector management are certain to yield greater efficiency, effectiveness, and accountability than are obtained from the kaleidoscopic attitudes and values reflected in the public-sector bureaucracy.

This prevailing attitude is clearly reflected in the pages of Vice-President Gore's *Report of the National Performance Review*.[1] The dominant theme emerging from this report is one of "bottom-line" pragmatism: the federal government must begin to utilize more extensively the managerial procedures of the private sector that are geared to the economically strategic impulses of the entrepreneurial spirit. Moreover, implicit in the report is the proposition that the president, his top-level cabinet officials, and, indeed, Congress must begin to reassess and reorder their notions of public service. And here we are faced with a conundrum: Is the magnetic and seemingly universal appeal of democracy—not just as a specific form of government, but as a way of life—the result of the economic persuasiveness of free-enterprise capitalism and its hallmarks of competition, profit, and efficiency, or is the success of our competitive, free-enterprise, economic system the result of the basic ethical-moral principles that are deeply ingrained in the fabric of democracy?

The Business of Government

To be sure, for most of the last half of the twentieth century, the United States has expended untold resources in attempting to "make the world safe for democracy." During this period, it has consciously attempted to infuse the non-Western nations of the world with the constitutional traditions and the legal, political, and economic systems that shape the processes of democratic governance. By the same token, however, if the notion of democracy and the democratic political processes it engenders are to be lauded as being intrinsically superior to the various other "isms" and the political systems they generate, a clear recognition of democracy's inherent ethical-moral values must be acknowledged. As the previous chapters have attempted to make clear, there are certain values unique to democracy that especially need to be nurtured and protected at that stage of the policy process when law becomes transformed into action. Despite the many valid criticisms of public-sector management processes and procedures contained in Vice-President Gore's report, there is an integral and unique relationship between public-sector management, ethics, and democratic values that desperately needs to be, not reinvented, but emphatically reaffirmed and widely proclaimed as fundamental to the purpose of democracy.

As noted earlier, the public bureaucracy's past performance in the implementation of policy can hardly be assessed as exemplary. Nevertheless, is it not reasonable to suggest that the haunting, implicit question advanced by the essence of democracy—"Am I my brother's [and sister's] keeper?"—is far more comprehensible to those public-sector careerists who reflect the moral sensitivities inherent in the notion of service than to the new centurions of the corporate sector whose sensitivities of democracy are deeply embedded in the pragmatic canons of profit, efficiency, and competitiveness?

Political history is noted for the ironies it generates, and the current mood endorsing a shift toward the "privatization" of policy implementation is no exception. For well over the past 100 years, public administrators have been admonished to adopt the techniques, to reflect the attitudes, and to embrace the philosophy of their private-sector counterparts. The drive for civil service reform that began in the wake of the Civil War was simply the opening salvo of a much more extensive and intensive campaign designed to shape the managerial operations of government in the image of the private sector.

The year 1887 marked the publication of a journal article entitled "The Study of Administration" by Woodrow Wilson,[2] who just the year before, had received his Ph.D. from The Johns Hopkins

University. As noted in chapter 1, he advanced an argument for an inherent dichotomy between politics and administration. The latter should be concerned only with the responsibility for applying apolitical and generic management techniques to the implementation of public policy.

Although numerous interpretations of Wilson's article have been advanced, there can be no question that it was primarily a reform piece written by a reform-minded academician. It was designed to fit into the mainstream of the considerable body of reform literature being generated at the time. The article itself had more symbolic than real impact,[3] and certainly the ideas Wilson expressed did not originate with him.

"The field of administration is a field of business," wrote Wilson. "This is why there should be a science of administration which shall seek to straighten the paths of government, to make its business less unbusiness-like." Such a science of administration was essential to improve "the organization and methods of our government offices" and to realize "the utmost possible efficiency at the least possible cost either of money or of energy."[4] These ideas did not reach the scholarly alcoves of the academic community immediately, but if what *The Nation* printed is any gauge, they had been issues in the popular press.

In the seven years preceding the publication of Wilson's article, *The Nation* maintained a steady drumbeat calling for "an honest and generally efficient and business-like conduct of the departments."[5] It demanded "a change which recognizes human nature in the transaction of Government business to the same extent and by the same arrangements as in private business."[6] People selected for administrative positions were to be chosen on the basis of "their business qualifications."[7] The publication lauded President Grover Cleveland for his firm insistence on "the rule of business principles," and saluted the *Galveston* [Texas] *News* and the *New Orleans Times-Democrat* for their strong support of "business-like efficiency and single-minded fidelity in the public service." The editors approved public administrators who were "business-like and thorough in their methods, and always to be trusted."[8]

Three months before the appearance of Wilson's article, *The Nation* cited the customs house and the post office as "the two great business establishments of the Government in New York City [that] are now conducted upon business principles." After expressing some disappointment in Cleveland's administration, the journal continued: "But, making all due allowances for these failures, it still remains true that he has established a firm foothold for the system of a business administration."[9] On 7 April 1887, two months before Wilson's article appeared, *The Nation* ran an editorial headed "Government on Business Principles," in which it praised Secretary of the Treasury Charles S. Fairchild for establishing "a great business institution." The appointment of Fairchild by Cleveland was, according to the editors, "a most notable extension of the system of conducting the affairs of the Government on business principles."[10]

That Wilson capitalized on the temper of his times in no way diminishes either the perceptiveness of his analysis or the long-term significance of his article. Businesslike management and the science of administration were in fact the central themes of a half-century of American public administration, from the 1880s to 1929. The impact of these themes can be judged by comparing the editorial tones of *The Nation* in the 1880s, noted above, to the official opinions reflected in the Harding administration by the first director of the Bureau of the Budget, Charles G. Dawes, as discussed in chapter 1.

Efficiency was clearly associated with costs during this period, and costs were directly related to the quality of management decisions. Indeed, one major thrust of the government reform movement throughout the United States from the 1880s to 1929 was centrally focused on infusing the administrative aspects of all governments —federal, state, and local—with the notions of efficiency and economy. In 1910, Congress authorized President Taft to establish a Commission on Economy and Efficiency, and the impact of this "E and E" movement in government circles was greatly influenced by such private-sector management scholars as Frederick W. Taylor in the United States and Henri Fayol in France. Decreasing cost curves were a priori evidence of efficiency and soundly based business administration methods. Management principles judged sound in the private sector were assumed to be just as sound for the public sector. The time-honored dictum of "he who governs least governs best" was modified to "he who governs least expensively governs best." As budget director, Dawes established the precedent for focusing on cost-reduction methods that were equated with efficiency.

In later administrations, efforts to perpetuate Dawes's perception of public-sector management persisted in a variety of forms. Charles Wilson, President Eisenhower's secretary of defense, who was the former head of General Motors, was succinct in proclaiming his perspective: "What's good for GM is good for America." President Kennedy brought in Robert McNamara, the CEO of Ford Motor Company, as his defense secretary, and McNamara turned the federal establishment inside-out by introducing planning-programming-budgeting systems into the public administrative lexicon. "Management by objectives" had its genesis in the private sector and, after being tested in the Department of Health, Education, and Welfare during President Nixon's first term, was formally extended to all federal departments and ten other agencies by presidential memo in 1973. Under the active tutelage of President Carter, zero-based budgeting, which had been widely utilized in the private sector as well as in some state and local governments (including the State of Georgia), was mandated for all federal departments and agencies in 1977. To be sure, each of these efforts was plagued by various complications that compromised their potential effectiveness, but the intent to ensure that the machinery with which to run government routine business must be similar to the machinery to run private routine business, as Charles Dawes would say, persists. Indeed, during the 1990s one of the key focal points of government reform for both the Clinton administration and Congress has been "performance management." Vice-President Gore's *Report of the National Performance Review* and Congress's passage of the Government Performance and Results Act of 1993 send clear signals that the private sector's corporate culture—with its emphasis on accountability to stakeholders (stockholders), customer satisfaction, performance measurement, strategic planning, and downsizing tactics—is to be the template for a twenty-first century government.

The obvious irony of this situation is that the efforts of more than 100 years to make the business of government more business-like have not been for nought. The federal bureaucracy has been reasonably faithful in its attempt to adopt the techniques and to reflect the attitudes of the private sector. Given the *political* environment in which it must operate, however, it has had to adapt to the pragmatic *political* realities of life. That is to say, it has been forced to adapt to a situation in which the "bottom line" is the greatest good for the greatest number (as defined by the ephemeral clustering of a transitory majority of self-interested minorities), and not the greatest benefit for the least cost, as was urged by the apostles of the science of administration movement or their latter-day disciples. As many corporate executives have learned to their dismay after accepting positions in the public sector, utilitarian and optimizing strategies are by no means synonymous. But neither are they mutually exclusive, and herein lies the *fundamental* paradox that exists between public and private administration. Public-sector managers are expected—by chief executives, legislators, and the body politic—to be efficient in their administrative capacities *and* effective in achieving the goals and objectives of the programs assigned to them. Moreover, they are expected to be responsible to their executive branch superiors *and* accountable to the appropriate legislative bodies *and* responsive to the needs of their clientele groups. Finally, they are expected to be dedicated to the standards of their professions *and* politically astute enough to appreciate the pragmatic political realities of life *and* committed fully to a life of service in the name of democracy.

In the ranks of the career civil service, individuals whose professional competence is lacking are, for the most part, gradually weeded out; individuals whose political astuteness is either uninformed or misinformed usually leave on their own accord; but individuals whose ethical-moral awareness of the purpose of democracy is either nonexistent or woefully immature are unlikely (unless they have engaged in illegal activity) to receive organizational signals of disapproval. Thus, the challenge seems clear. Rather than devising new operating procedures designed to infuse the public sector with the values of the private-sector business community, perhaps a new reassertion of the values and virtues of democracy should be directed not only from the top levels of government but also from the combined efforts of the nation's professional schools.

As noted at the outset of this volume, future professionals who are now being encouraged and trained to guide society in the twenty-first century must begin to develop an abiding sense of ethical consciousness in much the same manner that the pragmatists of the past have honed their skills so effectively. Unfortunately, the latter capability seems to be much easier to develop than the former, possibly because it is easier to "solve" the pragmatic equation (Who's glad? How glad? Who's mad? How mad?) than it is to confront the stark reality that the purpose of democracy extends far beyond the limiting parameters of competition, profit, and efficiency. One reason why public-sector professionals are apparently more inclined to adapt to the pragmatic demands of a pluralistic, self-interest politics than to the transcendent demands of an ethical-moral commitment to the common good is, at first glance, fairly obvious. The vague and amorphous character of the common good seemingly provides little practical utility in the day-to-day operations associated with policy implementation. There is a second reason, however, that works much more subtly in directing public-sector professionals to follow their pragmatic inclinations. If one can conceptualize the common good as "whatever is true, whatever is honorable, whatever is just, whatever is lovely, whatever is gracious, if there is any excellence, if there is anything worthy of praise, think about these things" (Phil. 4:8 RSV), then it should be apparent that pursuit of the common good requires serious reflection and intense discernment. To engage actively in such a process clearly reveals that the workings of the common good are much more complex than the pragmatic intricacies advanced by the new centurions. For this reason, the dynamics associated with the common good need to be discussed in detail.

An Imbalanced Continuum

If we begin with the assumption that every individual is a rational being, it follows that there are essentially two basic strategies that can be employed by public-sector managers in selecting the most favorable or fitting alternative to pursue. On the one hand, when confronted with a set of alternative choices for which accurate, timely, and relevant data concerning each alternative are readily available, the individual is in an excellent position to apply rational cost-benefit analysis and to select the alternative that yields the most favorable ratio, that is, the alternative that maximizes benefits and minimizes costs. On the other hand, one can be confronted with a set of alternative choices involving multiple, complex variables that do not lend themselves to such precise quantitative analysis; or a situation in which the critical resources (including time) needed to conduct a thorough comparative analysis are not available; or both. In this instance, one is forced to select the alternative that, for the time being, is satisfactory in meeting whatever basic specifications are required to achieve an outcome that can be defended as fitting—that is, as meeting the immediate needs of the given situation. While less rigorous than the "optimizing model" of comprehensive rational analysis (the root method), the "satisficing model" of incrementalism (the branch method) provides a logical method of dealing with decision situations involving a high degree of ambiguity and uncertainty.[11] Having said this, however, is there another dimension of managerial decision making that is ignored by these two basic strategies of decision?

Let it be assumed as a given that every individual is a rational being who seeks that which is perceived as "good" and avoids that which is perceived as "bad." Is it not also reasonable, therefore, to assume that every public manager aspires to serve in a harmonious organizational atmosphere in which a meaningful sense of purpose, a satisfying sense of substantive accomplishment, and a holistic sense of unity tend to create an organizational consciousness that can only be described in terms of some higher good? To be more specific, is there a common good capable of motivating public-sector administrators to seek problem-solving alternatives that may very well include noninstrumental, intangible, symbolic, and/or deferred benefits? Is it possible that a rational manager can, quite rationally, seek to pursue implementation strategies other than those based on the self-serving assumptions of instrumental, tangible, material, and immediate gratification? In raising these questions, however, the notion of "rational" choice needs to be viewed from a much more complex perspective.

For instance, if it can be assumed that every public-sector manager has the intrinsic *potential* ability to seek the common good, the converse must also be assumed as true—that is, every manager has the intrinsic potential ability *not* to seek the common good. That is to say, every civil servant enjoys the intrinsic potential ability *to decide* which alternative to follow. Thus, in the case of the 1986 *Challenger* space shuttle disaster, for example, NASA project managers were faced with a major dilemma. Originally scheduled to launch on

23 December 1985, the mission had suffered four postponements that moved the launch date to 28 January 1986. Weather conditions for that date were forecasted as clear but cold—a predicted 26°F at the 9:38 A.M. scheduled launch time. Engineers at Morton Thiokol, manufacturer of the space shuttle's solid booster, expressed serious reservations about the performance of the booster rocket at such low temperatures. Their concern was specifically focused on the integrity of the gasketlike seals (O-rings) that were integral to the performance of the booster. No engineering test data had been compiled for such low temperatures, and the minimum temperature at which the Thiokol engineers were confident of optimum O-ring performance was 53°F. One Thiokol engineer was asked by NASA project managers to quantify his concerns. He responded: "I said I couldn't. I couldn't quantify it. I had no data to quantify it, but I did say I knew it was away from the goodness [sic] of the current data base."[12]

For NASA officials, the choice was agonizingly clear. Should they announce a fifth postponement and wait for more favorable weather conditions? Or, in view of the fact that Thiokol engineers could not state unequivocally that the O-rings would not function properly at temperatures below 53°F, should they order the *Challenger* to be launched as scheduled? In the final analysis, "the goodness of the current data base" was disregarded, as was the "goodness" of the human data base, that is, the seven crew members of the *Challenger*. After the four previous postponements, the *Challenger* management team was acutely aware of the compounding budgetary and political costs they had already incurred. Viewed solely in terms of their own operational and/or personal self-defined interests, the costs of a fifth postponement loomed much greater and far more certain than the costs associated with the problematic risk of an accident. Similarly, the prospects of the certain and tangible benefits of a successful mission outweighed whatever benefits could be associated with another postponement. In this context, any notion of a higher or common good was certain to be obscured by the pragmatic realities of the self-serving good.

Of course, in theory, the alternatives that exist between seeking the common good and the self-serving good can be considered equally accessible. That is, each individual manager can freely choose to view every problem-solving situation in terms of a greater good, or in terms of the composite summation of self-serving operational and/or personal goods. It must also be recognized, however, that these choices represent a zero-sum situation in which the public administrator is faced with two alternatives that are mutually exclusive. The choice between deferred and problematic benefits, on the one hand, and immediate and certain operational benefits, on the other, cannot be pursued simultaneously, as was clearly evidenced in the *Challenger* case. Moreover, as one's choices extend over time, a pattern emerges. Consider, for example, the decision continuum diagrammed in figure 6.1.

For simplicity, the two extremes of the continuum are designated as representing the absolute common good (+) and the absolute self-serving good (−). If it can be assumed that every junior-level, public-sector administrator begins his or her professional career at the center point on the decision continuum diagrammed below, the shaded, midsection of the continuum can be viewed as representing the organizational process of decision making acculturation. Thus, in the

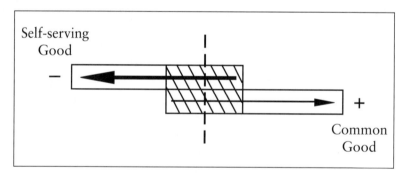

FIGURE 6.1

DECISION CONTINUUM

early stages of one's career, one learns the basic strategies of decision making associated with seeking either the common good or that good which, at the given moment, enhances one's self-defined interests.

Although it can be posited that every public-sector careerist begins his or her professional life at the center point on the decision continuum diagrammed in figure 6.1, experience informs us that the countervailing "magnetic" forces pulling in opposite directions along the continuum are by no means equal in strength. Thus, the proposition advanced here—as suggested by the thick, solid, arrowed line in the figure—is that the resultant "magnetic" force generated by the tensions of decision is heavily skewed or "loaded" to the downside or the negative pole of self-serving interests. Although it can be argued that the career public servant possesses the *intrinsic potential ability* necessary to overcome and counteract the natural pull of the "magnetic" negative, it also seems reasonable to suggest that, to overcome this attraction, an extraordinary degree of individual commitment, faith, and courage is required.

The primary force that "pulls" one to the negative pole of the decision continuum is the rational belief that the common good is derived from the realization of the aggregated self-serving goods. Thus, the deliberate intention to seek happiness and harmony through rational, individual, self-serving actions leads one further away from the positive pole of the decision continuum—the common good. The result, ironically, is that while each public-sector manager may yearn for all of his or her colleagues to share in a common state of harmonious well-being, the delusory power of the self-serving good causes the administrator to look for such organizational well-being in the wrong places.

The powerful pull of the negative pole generates visions of "the good society" in numerous bogus ways. The infatuation with personal and immediate gratification can be manifested through the attainment of power and status, honor and glory; through the pride that is derived from the aggregation of specialized "knowledge"; through the tangible attractiveness of the expansion of organizational resources; and, most significantly, through the pernicious innocence of habit. The self-serving good is a good that is easily disguised. It can be directed in a manner that is not only pleasing to the self but also to others, as well as to a larger community. Indeed, over time, (as was the case with President Eisenhower's secretary of defense, "Hot-Shot Charlie" Wilson) it is easy to become expert in rationalizing that what is good for one's own operational unit is good for the whole community or system.

This point can be extended to an even higher level. As noted before, Vice-President Gore's *Report of the National Performance Review* is intended "to make government work better and cost less." It promises to reinvent government through a "new customer service contract with the American people, a new guarantee of effective, efficient, and responsive government." Viewed in terms of short-term, tangible benefits, the report appears to be eloquent in its commitment to "the common good." Its more than eight hundred recommendations, if enacted, will save the nation's taxpayers $108 billion and will reduce the size of the federal civilian work force by 252,000. As a consequence, the downsized federal bureaucracy will develop a more cohesive, dynamic, and entrepreneurial spirit that will compete effectively with the private sector for the loyalty of its customers (i.e., citizens). Is it reasonable to ask, however, if such rhetoric, politically appealing as it may be, is directed to the common good or to the self-serving good presented in the guise of the common good? Clearly, the logic of the self-serving good is a compelling characteristic of being human, but, in fact, its value is realized only to the extent that it enhances one's ability to control and to manipulate the lives of others.

Given the powerful attractiveness of the self-serving (negative) pole of the decision continuum, and the absence of an equivalent countervailing force from the positive extreme (the common good), what possibility exists for the attainment of the common good? To focus on this question, one needs to move away from the purely rationalist theories of choice and consider the insights provided by a most unlikely source—the writings of St. Augustine.

For St. Augustine,[13] the answer rests solely in "the eye of the heart" of each individual, with the implicit axiomatic corollary that the capacity of the I's eye to "see" the common good is directly dependent on its *inability* to see itself. Thus, for Augustine, the primary function of the "eye of the heart" is to "see" the common good in its intended, unadulterated form of grace and love.

Rightly directed, the love ethic is always in service of the common good. Indeed, as seen by Augustine, everything created by God is good and can be loved, but how it is loved is the critical caveat.[14] This suggests, then, that it is the motive or the intent of one's love that determines one's ultimate movement across the decision continuum. The pathway to the common good demands considerable personal sacrifice with the hope of attaining a happiness and peace at some future point in time. It provides a sense of purpose that is eschatological in character. The alternative path offers disguised gratification, perverted notions of happiness and peace, and a deluded sense of "the common good." Infatuation with professional respectability and status is boundless and, despite one of Augustine's most frequently misconstrued dictums—"Love and live as thy wilt"[15]—professionals in the public sector would be well advised to heed another of his teachings, "Love, but see to it *what* you love."[16]

Indeed, the choice to follow the path to the self-serving good may be quite deliberate and consciously made; every public-sector manager is categorically free to reject the common good. But unlike the old Talmudic aphorism that advises "If you don't know where you are going, any road will take you there," Augustine seems much more resolute in his conclusion—if you don't know where you are going, you are inevitably destined to the eternal nothingness of the selfish, self-serving self. In a word, the psychedelic world of the self-serving self can easily become habit forming and dangerous to one's personal and organizational health.

Freedom to Forget

To coin a tautology, to the extent to which any aspect of daily life is habitual there is a natural tendency for it to become habituated —that is, to become a routinized, programmed, reactive, nonreflective response.[17] To be sure, much of human life is a composite of routinized, programmed responses—neurological and psychological —and most such habits are "valuable" in the sense that they enhance one's ability to behave "rationally."[18] Moreover, without a repertoire of habituated responses, organizational effectiveness would be seriously impaired. Paradoxically, however, the intrinsic value of such habituated routines is subject to what the economists would refer to as the law of diminishing returns. That is to say, the more routinized any aspect of life becomes, the less conscious awareness or significance is assigned to it. Thus, a serious question is raised: can the will to will the common good be nullified if that will has become effectively habituated by the routines satisfying the immediate demands of the self-serving good?

Admittedly, habit in organizational settings is indispensable. It provides a security derived from consistency, continuity, and predictability, and, most important, it provides relief from one's overburdened memory bank. The more aspects of one's organizational life that can be committed to habit, the less one has to store in memory. Thus, habit allows one not to have to remember, which is to say that it allows one to "forget" many of the less obvious aspects of choice.

Well-established operating routines, programs, and procedures provide every public-sector manager with ready guides to the inevitable question "What can I do?" As noted previously, a more fundamental dilemma involving every civil servant's ethical self centers around the ever-present decision-making challenge reflected in the question "What should I do?"[19] The answer to this latter question, as the *Challenger* project managers soon came to realize, depends on one's ontological self-perception. The manner in which one answers the basic ethical question—"What should I do?"—is determined by one's response to the basic ontological query, "Who am I?"

Unfortunately, as a result of the organizational habits acquired from pragmatic decision making and conflict-resolution strategies, most public administrators have either forgotten the significance of the question "Who am I?" or, even worse, they have lost all conscious awareness of the relational linkage it provides in addressing the other perennial question that is basic to the notion of public service: "Am I my brother's [and sister's] keeper?" From this, a grim irony seems to emerge. In lieu of the basic ontological query—"Who am I?"—which can no longer be answered because public managers have forgotten how to ask, a surrogate query is appropriated—"Who do people say I am?" As a consequence, day-to-day organizational existence for most public-sector careerists becomes a function of either doing what other people are doing, which is conformism, or doing what other people tell them to do, which is authoritarianism. In either case, something very precious is sacrificed in the public policy process without public managers being aware of its loss because habit turns the precious into the ordinary; it devaluates the valuable; it neutralizes that which is impassioned; and it reduces the distinctive to the nondescript. In short, the habits of a programmed, routinized choice process cause those who are responsible for ensuring that the laws are *faithfully* executed to sacrifice the passionate, invaluable, precious, and distinctive insights that can be derived from their interactions with the very citizens they are dedicated to serve—their neighbors.

In the context of democracy it is frequently stated that the gift of reason constitutes everyone's greatest freedom. Such a contention can only be viewed as ill conceived. Only the truly authentic self knows freedom. The decision-making "freedom" of reason that consumes organizational behavior is meaningless without a sense of the true freedom gained from an understanding of and commitment to the essence of democracy—namely, the common good. Only through a respect for and commitment to the common good can public servants learn who they really are. It is only in this mode that they can begin to develop the necessary relational linkages with their fellow citizens that permit public managers to feel completely free to act with authentic criticalness.[20] Thus, to the extent that they are able to effect this critical freedom, they are then in a position to recognize that unity through diversity is the essence of our democratic credo.

Public managers must recover the truly authentic and creative freedom to decide what they *should* do ethically in resolving the daily conflicts and challenges that confront them. Until they are capable of freeing themselves from the bondage of habit, any attempt to define professional behavior as truly ethical is an exercise in futility that can only result in pathetic self-deception. The habits of the self-serving good allow public servants to pursue a procedural, quasi-ethical life. The net result, to paraphrase H. Richard Niebuhr,[21] is a government of persons without fault, operating in a society without judgment, through the ministrations of a Constitution without a purpose. The grace of freedom *is* present always and everywhere. An awareness of this fact, however, *is not* present always and everywhere simply because so many administrators have forgotten the awesome responsibilities associated with such freedom. This sense of grace is removed from the organizational realms of critical consciousness by the habits of pragmatic and programmed operational behavior, and with it is also removed the critical freedom of public-sector managers to remember who they truly are. To reverse this condition of enfeebled democracy, public administrators must begin to remember that there is no freedom to be gained in their capacity to forget that they are their neighbors' servants.

As noted previously, the perennially haunting query, "Am I my brother's [and sister's] keeper?" is not an idle biblical soundbite. Most significantly, it is a fundamental question that goes to the heart of our democratic ethos. Who can disagree with Lincoln that democracy means "government of the people, by the people, for the people"? If reduced to its lowest common denominator, this inevitably translates into each citizen's responsibility for the well-being of his or her neighbor. A viable democracy rests on the basic assumption that the healthiness of the whole community depends on the wholesomeness of the relationships with each of its members.[22] Ironically, this notion, which is basic to twentieth-century systems theory, was also explicitly directed to the first-century A.D. Corinthians by the most prominent "entrepreneur" of his time, St. Paul.

Admittedly, the wizened wizards of pragmatic self-serving politics—the "new Corinthians"—who have shaped our management agendas for nearly the past fifty years do, in fact, advance a notion of communal unity. It is, however, of a significantly different character than that which St. Paul explained to his audiences: "The body is one and has many members, and all the members of the body, though many, are of one body.... If one member suffers, all suffer together; if one member is honored, all rejoice together."[23]

By contrast, the notion of unity advanced by many of the diverse voices we hear today tends to reverse this relationship. Namely, the whole body is honored to the extent that each member is free to act autonomously in maximizing his or her own self-interests. In the twenty-first century "Corinth," the prevailing social ethic is likely to sound very familiar to those who recall St. Paul's critical characterization of the first-century Corinthians: "because I am a foot and not a hand, or an ear and not an eye, I am not part of the body." Thus it follows, as noted by Paul, that in such a "body," the foot may say to the hand, or the ear may say to the eye, "I have no need of you."[24]

Twentieth-century America has not had a monopoly on diversity or complexity. Corinth, that unregenerate Greek city of friends, lovers, and other strangers, was a veritable mecca of rational "free choice" and diversity. Many of its citizens simply appropriated Christianity as a means to display an intellectual arrogance, a pretentious wisdom, and a misconceived presumption—that is, "all things are lawful for me."[25] Their notions of faith were linked to a sense of self-indulgent freedom of choice and expression—"Let us eat and drink, for tomorrow we die."[26] Is it forcing the point too much to suggest that the temper and tone of Corinth are with us still?

Pluralism is a given in any complex social reality. Paul spoke to the notion of a common good as the fundamental element needed to fuse a sense of unity from diversity.[27] A common good defined in terms of the grace of responsible freedom, however, runs diametrically opposite to a common good linked to the greatest number. Pluralistic diversity is the seedbed for reductionism and, as Viktor Frankl noted many years ago, "reductionism today is a mask for nihilism."[28] As public-sector organizations move into the twenty-first century, their search for operational "excellence" can, indeed, be found along the habituated pathways of rational, routinized behavior as defined either in terms of the greatest good for the greatest number or in terms of cost-benefit analysis. In the process, however, let us not pretend. Many of our notions of worthiness today are at about the same level they were in first-century Corinth.

If government *of* the people and *by* the people means anything at all, it means, first and foremost, that I, as a citizen, *am* my neighbor's servant. Thus, every citizen has a duty to serve the other, just as every public servant is, also, first and foremost, a citizen. Unfortunately, it should be apparent that the public bureaucracy has a dark side that can render career civil servants fundamentally incapable of perceiving, much less resolving, the ethical-moral dilemmas that inhere in virtually every decision-making situation. The reason for this lack of perceptive discernment relates, in no small degree, to the patterns of habit that cause administrators to forget the fundamental ethical-moral values and virtues that inhere in democracy.

A Centripetal Nexus

Like the people of Israel, the peoples of democracy are bound by a covenantal code. The value of the Exodus epic is found not as much in what it promises (freedom) as in what it requires (responsibility). All, not just some, citizens of democracy must also feel bound to these covenantal assumptions. Viewed in this context, the normative values inherent in democracy's sanctity of human freedom and dignity are mirrored in the holiness and wholeness tradition of the Exodus narrative.

In the context of public-sector organizations, the covenant of democracy is to remind civil servants of the close and constant vigilance required if the intricately devised system of democracy is to function effectively. It is also to remind them just how easy it is to lapse into habituated inattention, to forget the faithfulness which the day-to-day management of the political household requires, or to be lured by the wizened wizards of expediency into the programmed routines of reactive responses.

If public administrators are to move toward the common good, they must be prepared to manage our covenantal treasure of democratic values and virtues, not from the logic of reason alone, but from the "eye of the heart." Unfortunately, the values and virtues that infuse our democratic ethos have, over the years, been compressed into simplistic slogans by the passions of political rhetoric. As noted previously, the net result, so aptly described by Paul Ricoeur, has been "a ritualization of the moral life and a moralization of ritual."[29] That is to say, in our assiduous desire to exercise our "inalienable" freedom to forget, the fundamental ethical-moral covenant of democracy is erased from our historical and social memories.

Freedom, equality, and justice do, indeed, constitute the basic political values of our democratic commitment, but, with these three, there must be revived a fourth that lies fallow in our field of dreams, namely, responsibility. As applied to public management, the notion of professional responsibility is usually defined in terms of procedural obligations—for example, the obligation to adhere faithfully to legislative intent and the details of due process, the obligation to obey the law, and the obligation to recognize and respect the inviolability of organizational superior-subordinate relationships. If democracy, however, is viewed as a parabolic way of thinking about life in a community rather than as an institutional contrivance,* the notion of professional responsibility assumes a role of major proportions in our democratic equation.

---

* Robert Bellah et al. make essentially the same point in their book, *The Good Society* (New York: Knopf, 1991), 12. They refer to democracy

For example, professional responsibility represents a major factor in linking the other three fundamental political values (freedom, equality, justice) to a corresponding set of basic ethical values. In chapter 4 it was noted that Reinhold Niebuhr wrote, "practically every moral theory, whether utilitarian or intuitional, insists on the goodness of benevolence, justice, kindness, and unselfishness."[30] If taken literally as a universal statement, one may very well question the accuracy of this proposition. If, however, democracy, per se, is viewed as a "moral theory," as I would argue it must be, and if public-sector professionals are the critical moral agents of our democratic ideal, as I would contend they should be, the relevance of Niebuhr's proposition to our system of governance appears obvious. Our fundamental political values do, indeed, provide the basic amalgam needed to support our democratic system. That system, however, can become invigorated only to the extent that every career professional perceives freedom, equality, justice, and responsibility in terms of a personalized sense of benevolence, justice, kindness, and unselfishness. The critical linkage comes, however, not only in the fusion of these values, political and ethical, but also in the integral relationship that must be effected between these value sets and the moral *virtues* that form the essence of the common good.

Interestingly, our democratic political system traditionally has shown high regard for what are usually referred to as the cardinal virtues—prudence, temperance, fortitude, and justice.[31] Democracy demands its professional administrators to demonstrate good judgment, careful consideration, self-restraint, caution, and a balanced, well-developed sense of skepticism. The system demands *prudence*. It also places a high premium on moderation and a willingness to compromise in order to attain consensus and accommodation. The system demands *temperance*. Moreover, it requires a clear sense of direction, purposefulness, inner strength, mental discipline, and the

---

as a "metaphorical way of thinking about an aspect of many institutions"; I prefer to view democracy as a parable of history designed to guide individual human beings toward the common good.

ability to endure adversity with courage. It demands *fortitude.* Finally, it insists on the fair and equitable administration of laws, rules, regulations, procedures, and authoritative decisions in a decisive, dispassionate, and impartial manner. The system demands *justice.*

Unfortunately, history teaches us that these virtues, and the ethical values they engender, can be configured, by political officials and public administrators alike, in many self-serving, opportunistic fashions to meet the needs of diverse situations. If democracy is lucky, it can be governed and managed by individuals whose sense of prudence, temperance, fortitude, and justice is infused with the ethical values of benevolence, justice, kindness, and unselfishness, as well as the political values of freedom, equality, justice, and responsibility. But if democracy is unlucky—and that is at least an equal possibility—it can be governed and managed by individuals whose interpretations of these cardinal virtues, and the ethical and political values attached to them, are skewed in the most distorted manner. For example, Oliver North took great pride in his demonstration of fortitude; Richard Nixon always defended his political tactics as just; historians view Stalin as an extremely prudent national leader; and, to this day, the Neville Chamberlains of the world continue to counsel temperance.

Viewed from a political perspective, the key variable in linking together the two basic value sets is justice. Moreover, justice becomes the one cardinal virtue that gives meaning and balance to prudence, temperance, and fortitude. Nevertheless, it is essential to recall the warning of Reinhold Niebuhr: "Any justice which is only justice soon degenerates into something less than justice. It must be saved by something which is more than justice."[32] This is to say, none of the cardinal virtues can stand alone; they, too, need something more to support them if the political and ethical values they complement are to guide public administrators toward a mature vision of the common good.

The final components that are needed to create a dynamic system energized by a holistic ethical-moral perspective are the three foundational norms or virtues discussed in detail in chapter 4. To recall the propositions advanced previously, faith, complemented by trust, must be linked to an optimistic hope for the future of democracy. Both faith and hope, however, can become twisted caricatures unless infused with a completely unilateral love directed at the attainment of the common good by all servants of democracy. In the absence of such a sense of love or devotion to the common good, the entire system of democratic values and virtues stands as a teetering house of cards, easily tumbled and even more easily drawn into the "magnetic field" of the self-serving good.

What is being argued here is that public managers are caught in a vortex of past, present, and future pressures, commitments, and desires, and, as a consequence, the individual civil servant is inevitably fragmented by the centrifugal dynamics of pluralistic diversity. Caught in the midst of such a personal, social, economic, and political centrifuge, it appears that the "rational" administrator has no choice other than to follow the pathways of his or her own self-serving operational "good." As a consequence,

> the scale of the conflicts in which [the public servant] has to choose—with no advice or support except from his own conscience—tears him to pieces. Evil approaches him in so many respectable and seductive disguises that his conscience becomes nervous and vacillating, till at last he contents himself with a salved instead of a clear conscience, so that he lies to his own conscience in order to avoid despair.[33]

Given our capacity to forget, the ability to move toward the common good is no mean feat. It is simply not enough for public-sector managers and administrators to proclaim their commitments to the democratic values of freedom, equality, and justice and to expect these commitments to guide them through the variety amplifying maze of the public policy process. What is required of career professionals is a conscious awareness of the fact that these democratic values are vacuous unless linked by the force of self-responsibility to the personal ethical values of benevolence, justice, kindness, and unselfishness. Even if this happy confluence should result, however, public-sector careerists must reflect a clear recognition of the fact that the political and personal *values* of democracy ensure little more than the appearance of civility. The concept of justice must be consciously recognized as the primary and essential link that fuses our political and personal value base to the cardinal *virtues* of prudence, temperance, fortitude, and justice, on the one hand, and the foundational *virtues* of faith, hope, and love, on the other. Drawn together, these four sets of values and virtues create a centripetal nexus capable of guiding every civil servant to the common good. In short, the values of democracy are hollow vessels unless infused with the virtues of democracy, and the virtues are unattainable in the absence of the values. Viewed in this context, the common good becomes the *eschaton* of democracy. As such, it provides each public-sector administrator with a unifying sense of direction, an inspiring sense of purpose, and a loving sense of just-ness toward one's neighbor.

An Eschatological Vision

The primary challenge facing public administrators today is formidable. To what extent are they willing to manage the multiple inputs of objective and subjective freedom, quantitative and qualitative equality, procedural and substantive justice, and de jure and de facto responsibility? Moreover, to what extent are they prepared to relate this mixed set of dynamic variables to the ethical values of benevolence, justice, kindness, and unselfishness, as well as the cardinal and foundational virtues? The manner in which this complexity of variables is defined and configured by public-sector administrators will determine the extent to which our democratic system of governance is capable of (1) correcting disruption in the system, (2) preventing malfunctions before they occur, and (3) being directed toward a vision of the common good. The first function requires professional career administrators to respond with a *reactive* capacity; the second, an *anticipatory* capacity; and the third, a *transcendental*—that is, *eschatological*—capacity.

Given the essence of democracy, all three of these functions —correction, prevention, and direction—are integrally related. Unfortunately, given the rapidly accelerating rise in sociopolitical diversity and technoscientific complexity, these three functions have come to be viewed by many, if not most, public-sector professionals as mutually exclusive. As a result, the processes of democratic governance—including, especially, the administrative implementation of public policy—have become increasingly focused on the reactive and anticipatory functions (and in many instances solely on the reactive function) at the expense of the directional, that is, eschatological or goal attainment, function.

Reflecting on the continuing development of public administration, it seems reasonable to conclude that the eschatological ideals (or far goals) that energized our nation in its infancy have been gradually transformed into immediate and narrowly focused policy, programmatic, and operational ends. These, in turn, have been narrowed even more specifically to well-defined objectives, quotas, procedures, and performance measures during the past five decades. As a consequence, political, programmatic, operational, and/or professional survival can very well become the *only* goal, near or far, worthy of pursuit. After all, in the behavioral world of the eminent psychologist B.F. Skinner,[34] that which survives is worthy of survival.

If the eschatological vision of democracy is allowed to atrophy, a void is certainly created in the minds of civil servants. To be sure, all change proceeds in increments, however defined. Nevertheless, a fundamental distinction must be made between public-sector managers who move incrementally to embrace the values and virtues of democratic purposefulness, and those who view incrementalism as a pragmatic expedient and embrace it as an end in itself. For the latter group, those who do survive are considered survival-worthy, and, as a result of their efforts, the polity at large is directly affected. The rich do grow richer, the gap between the "haves" and the "have-nots" does continue to expand, and virtually all of the resources for governance at the disposal of democratic societies are directed toward the corrective and reactive functions needed to retain the status quo.

To coin another tautology, the primary purpose of democracy is, first and foremost, to define its purposefulness. What is it good for? What purpose does it serve? Interestingly, these were essentially the same questions that were posed repeatedly to Moses by the Israelites as they confronted the trials and tribulations of their exodus.

The common good is the promise of the Exodus covenant as well as the democratic covenant, and both provide the vision needed for statehood, citizenship, and historical purposefulness. Faithfulness and responsibility, the all-pervasive themes of the Exodus epic, are as worthy of our reverence today as when they were first imposed on the people of Israel. The faithfulness of our cadre of civil servants is certain to be challenged in the spheres of the contemporary wilderness. The costs that can be incurred in pursuing the common good can have substantial tangible and intangible negative impacts on the professional careers of those who choose to follow this path. Nevertheless, the tangible and intangible positive gains that can be realized in pursuing the common good can also be substantial not only for the individual public servants involved but also for the greater good of the larger community that may be involved. The joy of the journey, however, is gained from the wholeness and sanctity of the enterprise. The sense of human identity and democratic purposefulness embedded in covenantal unity—the common good—is, in itself, a truly revolutionary force not only capable of reinventing government but also of rededicating a nation to its authentic sense of being.

In reflecting on the notion of the common good as presented in this and the previous chapter, it should be apparent that the essence of its truly dynamic thrust is found in an eschatological vision that is fundamentally moral in nature. Unfortunately, we are frequently loath to acknowledge the moral dimension that permeates our bureaucratic-democratic ethos. Moreover, much of the current attention given to public-sector ethics is devoid of any moral relationship. If administration is law in action, then it seems apparent that ethics is morality in action. From this it follows that the ethical relationship between democracy and bureaucracy must be linked by a moral impulse. The ramifications of this proposition provide the focus of the concluding chapter.

7
The Moral Dimension
of Democracy

IN 1989 two noteworthy bicentennials were celebrated. One marked the formal establishment of the government of the United States of America; the other marked the formal establishment of the Catholic church in America.

It was in 1789 that the citizens of the original thirteen states finally faced the reality of a new government taking shape in both form and substance. As Edward Corwin succinctly put it:

> The first Wednesday of January 1789 was fixed as the day for choosing presidential electors, the first Wednesday of February for the meeting of the electors, and the first Wednesday of March [i.e., 4 March 1789] for the opening session of the new Congress. Owing to various delays, Congress was late in assembling and it was not until April 30, 1789 that George Washington was inaugurated as the first President of the United States.[1]

It was also in 1789 (November) that the first American Catholic diocese was formally established in the State of Maryland, with a Jesuit, John Carroll, being named as the first Catholic bishop in the United States. In his ecclesiastical position, Carroll—whose cousin, Charles Carroll, was a signer of the Declaration of Independence —symbolized the notion of religious freedom that was deeply embedded in the thinking of the Founding Fathers and the wording of the First Amendment to the Constitution.

More than a century and a half earlier, in 1634, another Jesuit, Andrew White, had arrived in Maryland after having been driven out of England by the Anglican church. At approximately the same time as White's arrival, a Huguenot family by the name of Dufour landed in Maryland, having been driven from France by the Catholic church.

These diverse bits of historical information reached an ironic point of convergence some 354 years after Andrew White and the Dufours arrived in Maryland. In 1988, Frank DeFord—direct descendent of the Dufour family, bona fide Protestant, celebrated sports journalist, author, screenwriter, and native of Maryland—was awarded the Andrew White Medal by the Jesuit President of Loyola College of Maryland. In accepting the award, DeFord commented:

> How ironic it is that the more open and integrated our society becomes, the more it is considered best—and safest—to segregate religion from society.... Today, religion is the only thing identified as different, and so the greatest religious intolerance in America today is directed at religion—not at Jews, not at Moslems or Mormons or Catholics, but at religion.[2]

Assume for the moment that DeFord was correct in his contention that intolerance toward religion, and the moral values it embodies, is prevalent today. What was the status of religion at the time of the founding of our nation? Did we encourage the development of institutionalized and denominational religions and, at the same time, eschew the manifestation of moral values in our daily lives?

What was ratified in 1788 was a Constitution plus an addendum—the Bill of Rights—that provided a framework for the governance of a nation and a set of restrictions designed to limit the use of such governing power. Thus, when George Washington was inaugurated as our first president in 1789, he assumed the responsibility for implementing the Constitution and the Bill of Rights, including, of course, the initial clause of our hallowed First Amendment freedoms: "Congress shall make no law respecting an establishment of religion, or prohibiting the free exercise thereof."

After more than 200 years of sifting through the historical records and documents of the constitutional birth of our Republic, historians have uncovered no evidence that the political or religious figures of that period misinterpreted the religion clause of the First Amendment. Certainly the intent of this clause was not lost on America's first Catholic bishop, John Carroll. Nor was it lost on America's

Protestant Episcopal bishops, the Methodists, the Congregational-ists, the Baptists, or the Presbyterians. Indeed, for all, the message was the same. Americans were free to engage (or not to engage) in the exercise of religion, but the federal government was mandated to ensure a clear separation between the public policy process and the formal institutional structures of religious denominations.

If George Washington and John Carroll could have been present in 1989 at their respective bicentennial commemorations, surely both would have applauded our nation's faithful insistence on main-taining a clear gap between church and state. Without question, however, both would have been appalled by the manner in which our post–World War II generations have interpreted this clause to en-sure a clear separation between an individual citizen's private moral values and his or her value-free, amoral public life. This, it would seem, is what DeFord was implying when he stated that "the great-est intolerance in America today is directed at religion"—that is to say, at the ethical values and moral virtues intrinsic to the notions of democratic governance.

At the time of the creation of our new Republic, the essence of that democratic experiment was deeply embedded in our Judeo-Christian heritage, and none of the Founding Fathers—even the most agnostic among them—was prepared to argue that a commit-ment to public service was to be devoid totally of ethical value or moral virtue. To suggest that a notion of public ethics should be viewed with an amoral detachment would, in all likelihood as Frank DeFord argued, leave the Founding Fathers "aghast—not just at our vulgarity, but at our temerity."[3]

To be sure, such an allegation may strike many as extreme, espe-cially those who have labored unstintingly in devising comprehen-sive legal-rational structures and procedures to ensure ethical behav-ior in the workings of governmental systems. What does it mean to suggest that such actions can be characterized as temerarious—that is, rash, reckless, contemptuous, audacious? It is a stern judgment, but the truth of the matter is that, although we strive desperately in our contemporary political rhetoric to maintain the pretense of a commonwealth, we consistently refuse to recognize what constitutes the essence of a commonweal. Specifically it can be asked if it is rash, reckless, contemptuous, even audacious to maintain the pretense that there is no direct historical correlation between the development of democracy and the relevance of ethical-moral values in striving for the attainment of the common good of democracy?

For example, it is certainly reasonable to equate ethics with justice, and to argue that our reverence for the law can be found in the rationality of its reason. As noted in chapter 2, however, while reason may explain our defense of the law, it does not explain our reverence. "The sense of justice," Reinhold Niebuhr observed, "is a product of the mind, not of the heart. It is the result of reason's insistence upon consistency."[4] In other words, is there more to ethics than the legal dimensions of *stare decisis?* Is there more to justice than the statutory stipulations of the law? Is there any contemporary relevance to be gleaned from the biblical passage,

> The aim of our charge is love that issues from a pure heart, a good conscience, and sincere faith. Certain persons swerving from these have wandered into vain discussions, desiring to be teachers of the law, without understanding either what they are saying or the things about which they make assertions.[5]

Possibly here lies the danger of our infatuation with a purely amoral rational-legal perspective of democracy. The more we attempt to legislate the structures and procedures of public-sector ethical behavior, the less we understand about the moral dimensions of an ethical life, and the more moral values become removed from the reality of the public policy process. At present, we are faced with an unprecedented, convoluted system of human values in which morality is stripped of substantive significance, ethics is detached from any moral connotation, and individual behavior is made ethical to the extent that it conforms empirically to the statutory directives of a rational legal order. Given the multiplicity of cases of ethical impropriety stemming from all levels of government over the past several decades, does it not seem fair to conclude that whatever is legal is ethical, and only that which is categorically illegal is unethical? If this is the case, how can we avoid the disturbing conclusion that

> In the hierarchy of values in today's world ... objective moral values ... are banished to the realm of the individual where they

merit no public defense from the community. There is, to put it bluntly, a right to act immorally but morality itself has no rights.[6]

If one is inclined to dismiss this comment as ultraconservative hyperbole, consider one that was made more than 350 years ago—indeed, about the same time that Andrew White was driven out of England and the Dufour family was expelled from France— by the English poet and social critic John Milton in his handbook on freedom of speech and expression, *Areopagitica:* "that which is impious or evil absolutely against faith and manners, no law can possibly permit." Viewed from today's self-enlightened, value-free, emancipated social order, with its focus heavily skewed toward the self-serving good, Milton's quaint and prosaic admonition can only earn our patient indulgence. Unfortunately, the previous quotation is closer to the truth. Faith, manners, and certainly morality have no rights; the only ethics that applies in the public square is that which the law defines and the courts interpret as legal behavior.

Possibly in an effort to abate the barren moral climate that has steadily engulfed the public sphere over the past five decades, the sub- ject of ethics has become one of the fastest-growing issues of interest in our society today. Virtually all political jurisdictions of any signifi- cant size are intensely involved in drafting, redrafting, and enforcing comprehensive codes of ethics designed to inform public-sector offi- cials and employees what they have to do to be ethical individuals in the course of their public duties and functions. These various over- tures might create the impression that a surge of ethical consciousness is sweeping through the ranks of public-sector organizations. As a re- sult of its procedural, mechanistic, and myopic foci, however, the sub- stantive impact of such ethical awareness frequently leaves much to be desired. The net result, all too often, is an ethics of compliance: tell me what is right, what is wrong, what is legal, what is not permis- sible; if there is anything free from blame, if there is any security from accusation, tell me about these things so that I can be judged an ethi- cal public servant. In short, we have, indeed, become assiduous in ritualizing the moral life and, in the process, we have become expert in moralizing the ritual. Viewed in this context, the inevitable and distressing conclusion is that the notion of an "ethical public service" increasingly appears to be a contradiction in terms.

When ethics is defined in terms of legalistic stipulations and procedures, it not only assumes a penal character but is also able to delight in the clarity of its precision. Placed in a context of what a majority of minorities defines at any given time as right or wrong, good or bad, the clarity of a codified body of ethics stands as a beacon of certitude. When in doubt, one should be able to determine the "correct" course of action simply by comparing the facts of any given situational dilemma to the applicable stipulations of the existing ethical code. Moreover, by limiting attention to the purely rational and empirical dimensions of the policy process, public-sector officials and administrators create an insular position for themselves designed to minimize, if not eliminate, the degree of personal ethical responsibility attached to virtually all complex decisions.

In any social system where ethical values are detached from their moral components, each individual is responsible only to ensure his or her own good and not the good of others, where "good" is defined as conformity to the law. In this context, therefore, prudence dictates that the only valid response to the question "Am I my brother's [and sister's] keeper?" is unequivocally no. In a strictly rational mode of legalistic ethics, the self-serving good becomes a paramount consideration. By the same token, the values of prudential pragmatism dictate that all decisions in the policy process be determined by the utilitarian calculus of consent. In this context, ethics becomes a calculable design that permits no inputs from the corpus of moral virtues. It is, however, from this source of moral virtues that democratic government derives its main justification for being. Indeed, regardless of how we may try to eschew the relationship between ethics and moral responsibility, the fundamental values and virtues of democracy are premised on the assumption that we are our brothers' and sisters' keepers. In this regard, the ethical values of democracy are essentially moral in nature. They give our democratic society a name, a face, an identity, and a character. Moreover, they give us a sense of purpose and a sense of direction. They give us a reason to live, just as, on occasion, they give us a reason to die.

An ethics derived from the pragmatic calculus of consent steers public servants toward the objective intent of ensuring a quantitative balance of interests, which we pridefully refer to as the pluralism of democracy. Viewed in this context, democracy is valued for the richness of its diversity as reflected in the basic quantitative measures of equality. What is overlooked, however, when viewing ethics from this perspective, is the fact that the richness of democracy's quantitative diversity becomes a viable factor only to the extent that it generates a qualitative sense of moral unity. In other words, ethics directly relates to the moral quality of democratic life; ethics delineates the breadth and depth of our fundamental democratic values and moral virtues; and ethics emphasizes the qualitative features of a moral sense of the common good.

At this point in our history, we seem to have lost sight of the fact that the quantitative dimensions of democracy are self-destructive mechanisms unless they are integrally related to the qualitative unity of the moral spirit of democracy. Our quantitative infatuation with cultural diversity—which we are quick to laud under the banners of individualism and toleration—has, in fact, generated an intense intolerance of any sense of qualitative unity, moral or otherwise. If it is true that the greatest intolerance in America today is directed at moral values, then any notion of a public ethic dependent on a sense of moral consciousness must be rejected categorically, not only as operationally dysfunctional, but as politically subversive. Each citizen who affirms this position must, then, be prepared to answer how far a tolerant society can go in its collective toleration of intolerance.

The question is not entirely academic. We have, as a united nation of states, become expert expositors of "the law" as a basis for ethical actions without understanding the nature of ethics as it relates to ourselves and others as moral human beings. On the other hand, perhaps we understand all too well the sense of personal responsibility that is attached to an ethical-moral consciousness, and we deliberately choose not to bear this personal burden. Indeed, this may very well constitute the true character of our own personal sense of intolerance. If Reinhold Niebuhr's contention that every moral theory insists on the goodness of benevolence, justice, kindness, and unselfishness is sound, does it not follow that, at the end of the twentieth century, most of what passes as contemporary social theory has little or no relationship to what Niebuhr refers to as moral theory?

Yet, as we enter the twenty-first century, we seem to be mesmerized by the notion of theory to the point where theory is the only reality countenanced by our society. In whichever policy arena a public manager happens to be situated, whether it is law enforcement, health care, education, housing, and so on, there is no dearth of micro, macro, or meta theories to distract attention from the empirical realities that reveal the slow but steady degeneration of ethical-moral values. Theory, not religion, has become the opiate of our society. Indeed, the ethical-moral "theories" advanced over the centuries by philosophers and theologians have been relegated to the dustbins in the cellar of the edifice constructed by the twentieth century's new "sciences" of social life. Ironically, however, as this century of behavioral science draws to a close, many of its acolytes are scurrying to reclaim ethics as an integral component of their respective behavioral models and theoretical constructs. But why, one can reasonably ask, is ethics relevant only if subsumed in the context of some existing social "science" theory? Are we somehow less intelligent, less rational, less feeling human beings if we do not have a theory to explain and direct our ethical-moral impulses? Does it follow that without the benefit of a theoretical framework, an ethics of morality can be cavalierly disregarded as a fantasized product of our opiated minds—a product of folklore, prejudice, or psychedelic happenings?

The truth of the matter is that the notion of an ethical-moral theory is something of a contradiction in terms. Reasoned debate, empirical research, and theoretical constructs will not resolve the anguished tension that inevitably manifests itself when we are forced to confront that which we *can* do with the desperate need to decide what we *should* do, or, even more disturbing, when we are called upon to view our neighbors through the eyes of love and the eyes of justice at the same time. To avoid such anguish, we are quick to embrace virtually any "theory" that seems to offer a definitive and comfortable escape from the moral challenge inherent in the eternal question "Am I my brother's [and sister's] keeper?" Viewed in this context, one can begin to understand what it means to say that theory is, in fact, the only reality countenanced by society.

Despite the intellectual rigor, precision, and rational certitude presumably associated with the process of theory building, the fact remains that the deeply rooted moral dimensions of democratic society are effectively disregarded and functionally distorted by most of

our elegant and sophisticated sociopolitical theories. As Michael
Walzer appropriately notes:

> Liberty, justice, democracy, domination, oppression, exploitation,
> cruelty, violence, terror, mass murder, totalitarian rule—this is the
> language of politics in the twentieth century, a time of large
> hopes, high risks, desperate efforts, fearful culminations. Who
> can doubt that this language is better employed by a person of
> moral sensitivity without a theory than by a morally obtuse per-
> son with the grandest possible theory.[7]

In the public sector, behind the codes of ethics, regulations, rules,
and procedures—all of which seem to expand exponentially—there
lies a "theory" that is as elegant in its simplicity as it is obtuse in its
moral comprehension: If you do not do that which is "wrong," you
must be "right." We can continue to perpetuate this grand theory of
procedural ethics and, at the same time, pride ourselves on the astuteness of our ethical sensitivity. We can, on the other hand, begin
to recognize that our sense of public-sector ethics is inextricably
linked to the moral essence of each individual citizen, as well as to
the fabric of democracy. In the process, we can then, also, begin to
recognize that justice, for instance, assumes a new dimension. It reveals a new horizon, not just of judgment but of love and compassion as well. Democratic and moral values are indivisible; they are
interwoven into a seamless garment. An ethics of moral consciousness insists on the fusion of ethical values and moral virtues. Democracy requires nothing more, but it certainly demands nothing less,
and a life so lived in the service of democracy reveals the genuine
worth of its noble calling.

The prophets and poets in the ancient histories of Israel and
Greece are remembered as noble figures who lived a life of service in
the name of their respective visions of a higher good. They were the
watchmen of their communities who applied the moral standards of
their higher good neither passively nor mechanically but with an
openly expressed sense of anger and critical consciousness. Given the
politically correct attitudes that prevail in our bureaucratic systems
today, how far can a passionately committed public servant follow
this critical pathway without becoming a stranger in his or her own

land, a prophet without honor, or even a dangerous subversive? To attempt to serve as a dynamic change agent in a system that seeks ethical correctness but eschews either an explicit or even an implicit commitment to the moral virtues that are imprinted in democracy is to follow a path where angels fear to tread. The prophetic change agents of Israel and Greece were judicious interpreters of the public policies and social practices promulgated in their day. Their primary responsibility was to ensure that the social patterns resulting from these policies and practices provided firm hand rails to a higher good, as opposed to a slippery slope to a self-serving good. In this regard, there was no mistaking their role as "public servants." Their firm judiciousness was derived from a transcendent spirit of moral goodness, not from a procedural code of ethical correctness; from a sense of passion, not detachment. It reflected a categorical commitment to a common good that was not qualified by the self-serving sidesteps of prudential pragmatism. Their sense of justice was deeply embedded in the just-ness of love as exemplified in their pedagogical interactions with their neighbors, as well as strangers. Their sense of courage was that of the lion, not of the fox. Viewed in retrospect, the model of public service they defined loses none of its relevance or urgency as we prepare to advance democracy into a new century. The question facing us today is—as it was then—is anybody listening?

Notes

Introduction

1. David Osborne and Ted Gaebler, *Reinventing Government: How the Entrepreneurial Spirit Is Transforming the Public Sector from Schoolhouse to Statehouse, City Hall to the Pentagon* (Reading, Mass.: Addison Wesley, 1992); and David Osborne and Peter Plastrik, *Banishing Bureaucracy: The Five Strategies for Reinventing Government* (Reading, Mass.: Addison Wesley, 1997).

2. Osborne and Gaebler, *Reinventing Government,* xix; and Osborne and Plastrik, *Banishing Bureaucracy,* 14.

Chapter 1. Rediscovering Democracy — Is Anybody Listening?

1. "A Model of Christian Charity." Sermon delivered aboard the *Arbella,* 1630. See Perry Miller, ed., *The American Puritans* (New York: Doubleday, 1956), 82.

2. Robert Maranto, "Thinking the Unthinkable in Public Administration: A Case for Spoils in the Federal Bureaucracy," *Administration and Society* 29, no. 6 (January 1998).

3. See James W. Fesler, *American Public Administration: Patterns of the Past,* PAR Classics Series (Washington, D.C.: American Society for Public Administration, 1982), 7–8.

4. See Luther Gulick and Lionel Urwick, eds., *Papers on the Science of Administration* (New York: Institute on Public Administration, 1937).

5. Woodrow Wilson, "The Study of Administration," *Political Science Quarterly* 2 (1887).

6. Charles G. Dawes, *The First Year of the Budget of the United States* (New York: Harper and Brothers, 1923), 168.

7. Ibid., 171, 178.

8. Charles Lindblom and David Braybrooke, *The Strategy of Decision* (New York: Free Press, 1963), 190.

9. Charles Lindblom, *The Intelligence of Democracy* (New York: Free Press, 1965), 215.

10. Walter Kaufmann, ed., *Existentialism from Dostoevsky to Sartre* (New York: Meridian Books, 1957), 22.

11. H.H. Gerth and C. Wright Mills, eds., *From Max Weber: Essays in Sociology* (New York: Oxford University Press, 1946), 229.

12. *Public Papers of the Presidents of the United States: Lyndon B. Johnson,* Book II (25 August 1965).

13. Earl Latham, *Employment Forum* (April 1947), 6.

14. Donald Menzel, "Teaching Ethics and Values in Public Administration: Are We Making a Difference?" *Public Administration Review* 57, no. 3 (May/June 1997): 224–30.

15. Rain Jahanbegloo, "Philosophy and Life: An Interview" [with Isaiah Berlin], *New York Review,* 28 May 1992, 51.

Chapter 2. The Dark Specter of Hypocrisy and Pretense

1. Dwight Waldo, "Democracy, Bureaucracy, and Hypocrisy," A Royer Lecture (Berkeley: Institute of Governmental Studies, University of California, 1977), 16.

2. Dwight Waldo, *The Enterprise of Public Administration* (Novato, Calif.: Chandler and Sharp, 1980), 45.

3. Waldo, "Democracy, Bureaucracy, and Hypocrisy," 18.

4. Chris Argyris, "Making the Undiscussable and its Undiscussability Discussable," *Public Administration Review* 40, no. 3 (May/June 1980): 205.

5. Matthew 23:13–32 (RSV).

6. Paul Ricoeur, "Guilt, Ethics, and Religion," in *Moral Evil under Challenge,* ed. Johannes B. Metz (New York: Herder and Herder, 1971), 16.

7. Herman Finer, "Administrative Responsibility in Democratic Government," *Public Administration Review* 1, no. 4 (Summer 1941): 336.

8. Jerome Frank, *If Men were Angels: Some Aspects of Government in a Democracy* (New York: Harper and Brothers, 1942), 3–7; emphasis added.

9. Reinhold Niebuhr, *Moral Man and Immoral Society* (New York: Scribner's, 1932), 37.

10. Ibid., 258.

11. Mary Parker Follett, *Creative Experience* (New York: Peter Smith, 1951), 287–88, 52. Originally published by Longmans, Green, New York, 1924.

12. Perry Miller, *Errand into the Wilderness* (Cambridge, Mass.: Harvard University Press, 1964).

13. J.R. McCallum, *Abelhard's Christian Theology* (Oxford: Blackwell, 1948), 4.

14. Miller, *Errand into the Wilderness,* 7–8.

15. Alexis de Tocqueville, *Democracy in America* (New York: Vintage Books, 1964), 172–73; emphasis added. See also Louis C. Gawthrop, "The Ethical Foundations of American Public Administration," *International Journal of Public Administration* 16, no. 2 (1993).

16. Quoted in Richard Brookhiser, "A Man on Horseback," *Atlantic Monthly,* January 1996, 64.

17. Sydney E. Ahlstrom, *A Religious History of the American People* (New York: Image Books, 1975), 1:439–40.

18. Quoted in ibid., 468.

19. Quoted in ibid., 444.

20. Quoted in ibid., 166.

21. Waldo, *Enterprise of Public Administration,* 17, 24–25.

22. Louis C. Gawthrop, "Grail Hunting, Dragon Slaying, and Prudent Resilience: The Quest for Ethical Maturity," *Public Administration Quarterly* 13, no. 4 (Winter 1990): 528–30.

23. Quoted in Lionel Trilling, *Sincerity and Authenticity* (New York: Harcourt, Brace, 1980), 118.

24. Jeremiah 10:5 (RSV).

25. Viktor Frankl, "Reductionism and Nihilism," in *Beyond Reductionism,* ed. Arthur Koestler and J.R. Smythies (Boston: Beacon Press, 1971), 402.

26. This point is developed in more detail in chapter 6.

27. Herbert A. Simon, *The Sciences of the Artificial,* 3d ed. (Cambridge, Mass.: MIT Press, 1996), 188–89.

28. Dietrich Bonhoeffer, *Ethics* (New York: Macmillan, 1955), 191; emphasis added.

29. Dorothy Sayers, *Christian Letters to a Post-Christian World* (Grand Rapids, Mich.: William B. Eerdmans, 1969), 7.

30. Trilling, *Sincerity and Authenticity,* 172.

31. T. Bailey Saunders, ed. and trans., *Complete Essays of Schopenhauer* (New York: Wiley, 1942), 96–97.

32. Graham Greene, *The Quiet American* (New York: Penguin Books, 1977), 37.

33. Sayers, *Christian Letters to a Post-Christian World,* 152.

34. Trilling, *Sincerity and Authenticity,* 13.

35. Quoted in ibid., 5.

36. *Timon of Athens,* IV, iii.

37. Alasdair MacIntyre, *After Virtue* (Notre Dame: University of Notre Dame Press, 1981), 217.

38. Trilling, *Sincerity and Authenticity*, 78.
39. Miller, *Errand into the Wilderness*, 13.
40. MacIntyre, *After Virtue*, 200–201.

Chapter 3. Bureaucracy and the American Character

1. Alexis de Tocqueville, *Democracy in America* (New York: Vintage Books, 1964), 172.

2. Edward S. Corwin, ed., *The Constitution of the United States: Analysis and Interpretation* (Washington, D.C.: Government Printing Office, 1953), xix.

3. Carl B. Swisher, *American Constitutional Development* (Boston: Houghton Mifflin, 1954), 52.

4. Robert Goldwin, "Of Men and Angels: A Search for Morality in the Constitution," in *The Moral Foundation of the American Republic,* ed. Robert H. Horwitz (Charlottesville: University of Virginia Press, 1977), 8.

5. Leonard D. White, *The Federalists* (New York: Macmillan, 1948), 470–71.

6. Ibid., 472–73.

7. Swisher, *American Constitutional Development*, 23, 51.

8. *The Nation*, 28 May 1868, 425.

9. Ibid., 11 November 1880, 336.

10. Ibid., 272.

11. Leonard D. White, *The Jacksonians* (New York: Macmillan, 1954), 6.

12. Swisher, *American Constitutional Development*, 372.

13. Ibid., 374.

14. Leonard D. White, *The Republican Era* (New York: Macmillan, 1958), 4. See also William Hesseltine, *Ulysses S. Grant: Politician* (New York: Dodd, Mead, 1935), 339.

15. Samuel Morison and Henry Steele Commager, *The Growth of the American Republic,* 5th ed. rev. (New York: Oxford University Press, 1950), 1:278.

16. Ibid., 522.

17. Ibid., 520.

18. Esmond Wright, *Fabric of Freedom* (New York: Hill and Wang, 1978), 216.

19. Quoted in Richard Brookhiser, "A Man on Horseback," *Atlantic Monthly,* January 1996, 64. See also White, *The Federalists*, 258.

20. Leonard D. White, *The Jeffersonians* (New York: Macmillan, 1951), 246, 248–49, 264.

21. Ibid., 303.

22. White, *The Jacksonians*, 102–3.

23. Ibid., 184–85.

24. White, *Republican Era*, 243.

25. Ibid., 247–51.

26. Ibid., 242.

27. Lionel Trilling, *Sincerity and Authenticity* (New York: Harcourt, Brace, 1980), 38.

28. Proverbs 3:9–10 (RSV).

29. White, *The Jeffersonians*, 549.

30. Proverbs 3:3 (RSV).

31. Norton Long, "Bureaucracy and Constitutionalism," *The Polity* (Chicago: Rand McNally, 1962), 71–72.

32. David M. Levitan, "Political Ends and Administrative Means," *Public Administration Review* 3 (Autumn 1943): 359.

33. White, *The Federalists*, 268.

34. White, *The Jeffersonians*, 6.

35. Swisher, *American Constitutional Development*, 122.

36. Herman Finer, "Administrative Responsibility in Democratic Government," *Public Administration Review* 1 (Autumn 1941): 338.

37. Trilling, *Sincerity and Authenticity*, 109.

38. Libertus A. Hoedemaker, *The Theology of H. Richard Niebuhr* (Philadelphia: Pilgrim Press, 1970), 70. See also H. Richard Niebuhr, *The Responsible Self* (New York: Harper and Brothers, 1963), 83–85.

39. Trilling, *Sincerity and Authenticity*, 117.

40. John K. Roth, ed., *The Philosophy of Josiah Royce* (New York: Thomas Crowell, 1971), 278–80.

41. Trilling, *Sincerity and Authenticity*, 77.

42. *Plato's Republic*, trans. B. Jowett (New York: Random House Modern Library, n.d.), IX: 360.

43. Dwight Waldo, *The Enterprise of Public Administration* (Novato, Calif.: Chandler and Sharp, 1980), 45.

Chapter 4. The Spirit of Public Service

1. Exodus 10:12–27 (RSV).

2. Gustav Gilbert, *The Constitutional Antiquities of Sparta and Athens* (London: Swan Sonnenschien and Company, 1895), 220–22. See also Lewis Packard, *Morality and Religion of the Greeks* (New Haven: Tuttle and Taylor, 1881), 20–21.

3. B. Lyon, "What Makes a Medieval King Constitutional?" in *Essays*

in Medieval History, ed. T.A. Sandquist and M.R. Powicke (Toronto: University of Toronto Press, 1969), 162.

4. H. Richard Niebuhr, *Radical Monotheism and Western Culture* (New York: Harper and Row Torchbooks, 1970), 25.

5. Ibid.

6 Genesis 37–47 (RSV).

7. Gerhard von Rad, *Old Testament Theology* (New York: Harper and Row, 1965), 432.

8. Lawrence Boadt, *Reading the Old Testament* (New York: Paulist Press, 1984), 369.

9. Ibid.

10. Jeremiah 44:15–18 (RSV).

11. Marvin Becker, "Aspects of Lay Piety in Early Renaissance Florence," in *The Pursuit of Holiness in Medieval and Renaissance Religion,* ed. Charles Trinkaus (Leiden: E.J. Brill, 1974); and Daniel R. Lesnick, *Preaching in Medieval Florence* (Athens: University of Georgia Press, 1989).

12. Lesnick, *Preaching in Medieval Florence,* 30–34.

13. Becker, "Aspects of Lay Piety in Early Renaissance Religion," 190–91.

14. Ibid., 194.

15. Ibid., 196.

16. Ibid., 198.

17. Ibid., 177.

18. Exodus 10:12–27 (RSV).

19. Martin Landau and Russell Stout Jr., "To Manage Is Not to Control," *Public Administration Review* 39, no. 2 (March/April 1979).

20. Richard Neustadt, *Presidential Power* (New York: Wiley, 1980).

21. Paul Ricoeur, *The Symbolism of Evil* (Boston: Beacon Press, 1967), 135.

22. Stanley Hauerwas, *Against the Nations* (Minneapolis: Winston Press, 1967), 54.

23. Libertus A. Hoedemaker, *The Theology of H. Richard Niebuhr* (Philadelphia: Pilgrim Press, 1970), 71.

24. Reinhold Niebuhr, *Moral Man and Immoral Society* (New York: Scribner's, 1932), 258.

25. John Burnaby, ed., *Augustine: Later Works* (Philadelphia: Westminster Press, 1955), 298.

26. John le Carré, *The Honourable Schoolboy* (New York: Bantam Books, 1979), 461.

27. Mary Parker Follett, *Creative Experience* (New York: Peter Smith, 1951), chap. 10. Originally published by Longmans, Green, New York, 1924.

28. St. Augustine, "Enarrationes," *Nicene and Post-Nicene Fathers* (New York: Christian Literature Company, 1894), vol. VII, psalm LI.

29. H. Richard Niebuhr, *Radical Monotheism and Western Culture,* 103.

30. Michael Walzer, *Exodus and Revolution* (New York: Basic Books, 1985), 67.

31. St. Augustine, *The City of God* (New York: Penguin Classics, 1984), 873–74.

32. Leonard D. White, *The Federalists* (New York: Macmillan, 1948), 478.

33. Herbert Simon, Donald Smithburg, and Victor Thompson, *Public Administration* (New Brunswick, N.J.: Transaction Publishers, 1991), 8.

34. James Q. Wilson, *Bureaucracy: What Government Agencies Do and Why They Do It* (New York: Basic Books, 1989).

35. Frank Rourke, "Book Reviews," *Journal of Public Administration Research and Theory* 1, no. 1 (1991): 94.

36. T.S. Eliot, *Murder in the Cathedral* (London: Faber and Faber, 1938), 78–79.

37. For other historical assessments of the Federalist, Progressive, and New Deal periods, see Brian J. Cook, *Bureaucracy and Self-Government* (Baltimore: Johns Hopkins University Press, 1996); Gary C. Bryner and Dennis L. Thompson, eds., *The Constitution and the Regulation of Society* (Provo, Utah: Brigham Young University, 1988); Louis C. Gawthrop, "Grail Hunting, Dragon Slaying, and Prudent Resilience: The Quest for Ethical Maturity in American Public Administration," *Public Administration Quarterly* 13, no. 4 (Winter 1990); and idem, "The Ethical Foundations of American Public Administration," *International Journal of Public Administration* 16, no. 2 (1993).

38. Reinhold Niebuhr, *Moral Man and Immoral Society* (New York: Scribner's, 1932), 27.

39. Lionel Trilling, *Sincerity and Authenticity* (New York: Harcourt, Brace, 1980), 82.

Chapter 5. A Vision of the Common Good

1. Quoted in Sidney Baldwin, *Poverty and Politics* (Chapel Hill: University of North Carolina Press, 1968), 47.

2. Harold Laski, *The American Presidency* (New York: Harper and Brothers, 1940) 270–71; emphasis added.

3. Arthur Schlesinger Jr., *The Crisis of the Old Order* (Boston: Houghton Mifflin, 1957), 195.

4. Baldwin, *Poverty and Politics,* 268.

5. Arthur Schlesinger Jr., *The Coming of the New Deal* (Boston: Houghton Mifflin, 1959), 72.

6. Baldwin, *Poverty and Politics,* 76; and Schlesinger, *Coming of the New Deal,* 74–75.

7. Schlesinger, *Coming of the New Deal,* 77–80.

8. Baldwin, *Poverty and Politics,* 87.

9. Ibid., 84.

10. Ibid., 87.

11. F. Jack Hurley, *Portrait of a Decade* (Baton Rouge: Louisiana State University Press, 1972), 31–32.

12. Schlesinger, *Coming of the New Deal,* 369.

13. Ibid., 371.

14. Baldwin, *Poverty and Politics,* 92–93.

15. Ibid., 102.

16. Ibid., 163, 164.

17. Ibid., 107.

18. Ibid., 117.

19. Ibid.; emphasis added.

20. Karen Becker Ohrn, *Dorothea Lange and the Documentary Tradition* (Baton Rouge: Louisiana State University Press, 1980), 233.

21. Ibid., 223.

22. Ibid., 24.

23. Milton Meltzer, *Dorothea Lange: A Photographer's Life* (New York: Farrar, Straus and Giroux, 1978), 94–95.

24. Ibid., 97.

25. Ibid., 101.

26. Ibid., 132–33.

27. Ibid., 133.

28. Ibid., 133–34.

29. Baldwin, *Poverty and Politics,* 164.

30. Meltzer, *Dorothea Lange,* 155.

31. Ibid., 158.

32. Ibid., 163.

33. Ibid., 175.

34. Ibid., 203.

35. Ibid.

36. Ibid., 103.

37. Ibid., 229.

38. Ibid., 230.

39. Baldwin, *Poverty and Politics,* 267.

40. Ibid., 419.

41. Schlesinger, *Coming of the New Deal,* 371.

Chapter 6. Democracy, Bureaucracy, and the Common Good

1. Al Gore, "Creating a Government That Works Better and Costs Less," *Report of the National Performance Review* (Washington, D.C.: Superintendent of Documents, September 1993).

2. Woodrow Wilson, "The Study of Administration," *Political Science Quarterly* 2 (June 1887).

3. See Paul P. Van Riper, "The American Administrative State: Wilson and the Founders—An Unorthodox View," *Public Administration Review* 43, no. 6 (November/December 1983).

4. Wilson, "Study of Administration," 197.

5. *The Nation*, 11 November 1880, 336.

6. Ibid., 17 March 1881, 180.

7. Ibid., 19 December 1881, 506.

8. Ibid., 13 August 1885, 128.

9. Ibid., 10 March 1887, 202.

10. Ibid., 7 April 1887, 288.

11. See Herbert A. Simon, *Administrative Behavior* (New York: Macmillan, 1946). See also Charles E. Lindblom, "The Science of Muddling Through," *Public Administration Review* 19, no. 2 (Spring 1959).

12. *Report of the Presidential Commission on the Space Shuttle "Challenger" Accident* (Washington, D.C.: Government Printing Office, 6 June 1986).

13. St. Augustine, *The City of God* (New York: Penguin Classics, 1984), 1084.

14. Ibid., 636.

15. John Burnaby, ed., *Augustine: Later Works* (Philadelphia: Westminster Press, 1955), 252, 316.

16. Anders Nygren, *Agape and Eros,* trans. Philip S. Watson (Chicago: University of Chicago Press, 1982), 495.

17. Simon, *Administrative Behavior,* 88–89.

18. James G. March and Herbert A. Simon, *Organizations* (New York: Wiley, 1958), chap. 9.

19. Louis C. Gawthrop, "Ethics and Democracy: A Call for 'Barefoot Bureaucrats,'" monograph (Rotterdam: Erasmus University, 1993), 3.

20. Mary Parker Follett, *Creative Experience* (New York: Peter Smith, 1951), 130. Originally published by Longmans, Green, New York, 1924.

21. H. Richard Niebuhr, *The Kingdom of God in America* (New York: Harper and Brothers Torchbooks, 1959), 193.

22. John Dunn, ed., *Democracy: The Unfinished Journey* (New York: Oxford University Press, 1992), 240–43.

23. 1 Corinthians 12:26 (RSV).

24. Ibid., 12:16, 21.

25. Ibid., 6:12, 10:23.

26. Ibid., 15:32.

27. Ibid., 12:7.

28. Viktor Frankl, "Reductionism and Nihilism," in *Beyond Reductionism*, ed. Arthur Koestler and J.R. Smythies (Boston: Beacon Press, 1971), 398.

29. Paul Ricoeur, *The Symbolism of Evil* (Boston: Beacon Press, 1967), 135.

30. Reinhold Niebuhr, *Moral Man and Immoral Society* (New York: Scribner's, 1932), 27.

31. Gawthrop, "Ethics and Democracy," 10.

32. Reinhold Niebuhr, *Moral Man and Immoral Society*, 258.

33. Dietrich Bonhoeffer, *Letters and Papers from Prison* (New York: Macmillan, 1967), 3.

34. B.F. Skinner, *Beyond Freedom and Dignity* (New York: Knopf, 1971), 136.

Chapter 7. The Moral Dimension of Democracy

1. Edward S. Corwin, ed., *The Constitution of the United States: Analysis and Interpretation* (Washington, D.C.: Government Printing Office, 1953), 15.

2. Frank DeFord, "A Coalition of Friendly Strangers," *Loyola College Alumni Magazine*, Baltimore, November 1988, 18–19.

3. Ibid., 19.

4. Reinhold Niebuhr, *Moral Man and Immoral Society* (New York: Scribner's, 1932), 29. Also see 258.

5. 1 Timothy 1:5–6 (RSV).

6. Cardinal Joseph Ratzinger, *Origins* 18 (23 March 1989): 41.

7. Michael Walzer, *The Company of Critics* (New York: Basic Books, 1988), 88.

Acknowledgments

THIS brief volume represents a point of convergence, as well as a logical extension of my persistent attraction to a most noble profession, namely, public service. Many of the themes and concepts advanced in these pages underwent long periods of gestation. Moreover, my own thinking on the subject of public service in the spirit of democracy has been enriched, invigorated, and instructed by numerous challenging encounters along the way with a large number of professional practitioners, scholars, colleagues, and friends representative of diverse disciplines and interests. Whether it is apparent or not, this volume was greatly enhanced by their comments, insightful, gracious, and constructive.

Many of the central themes presented in the chapters that follow were initially advanced in other forums. With the passage of time, however, the focus of these themes has been expanded, refined, and/or revised, extensively in some instances, moderately in others. I extend my sincere appreciation and grateful acknowledgment to the publications in which these themes were initially presented: "Why Teach Ethics?" *Perspectives on the Professions* 7, no. 2 (January 1988); "Bureaucracy and Constitutional Development: The Duty to Risk," in *The Constitution and the Regulation of Society*, ed. Gary C. Bryner and Dennis L. Thompson (Provo, Utah: Brigham Young University Press, 1988); "Ethics and Democracy: The Moral Dimension," *Journal of State Government* 62, no. 5 (September/October 1989); "Images of the Common Good," *Public Administration Review* 53, no. 6 (November/December 1993); "Public Management and the Common Good," *Professional Ethics* 3, no. 1 (1994); "In the Service of Democracy," *International Journal of Public Administration* 17, no. 12 (1994); "Democracy, Bureaucracy, and Hypocrisy *Redux*: A Search for Sympathy and Compassion," *Public Administration Review* 57, no. 3 (May/June 1997).

To a very real extent, this volume—indeed, all my work—is a collaborative effort involving one who is endowed with boundless grace and infinite patience. Her advice and counsel over the years have enabled me to avoid many pitfalls. My obstinacy has caused me to incur many others that could have been avoided. In so many ways, this volume is as much the result of her efforts as it is mine.

Finally, a note of profound sadness envelopes this volume. I met with Ed Artinian at a professional conference in Washington, D.C., in August 1997 and delivered to him the initial manuscript copy of this work. He put the manuscript in his briefcase and, in his usual convivial manner, said how he was looking forward to a vacation following the end of the conference. Less than two weeks later, Ed Artinian died suddenly, and surely his loss has affected all who were drawn into his orbit. Several months later, Pat Artinian and I reestablished contact, thus beginning the long and tedious process that brings a manuscript to publication. Needless to say, we both were saddened by the circumstances that brought us together, but I felt privileged by the association. Her steady composure, gracious manner, and critical judgment are hallmarks of the Chatham House imprint.

Subsequently, Bob Gormley and Ted Bolen assumed the leadership of Chatham House Publishers. They are fully committed to the values and visions that Ed Artinian applied so successfully throughout his professional career. I wish them well in their new undertaking and can only hope that this brief volume can contribute to the illustrious beginning of a new chapter in the Chatham House legacy.

Index

About the Author

Louis C. Gawthrop is Eminent Scholar and Professor of Government and Public Administration at the University of Baltimore. In 1998 he received the American Political Science Association's John Gaus Award "honoring the recipient's lifetime of exemplary scholarship in the joint tradition of political science and public administration."

Dr. Gawthrop received his B.A. degree from Franklin and Marshall College, his M.A. and Ph.D. degrees in political science from The Johns Hopkins University, and his Master of Divinity degree from the Weston School of Theology, Cambridge, Massachusetts. He has taught at Indiana University–Bloomington, the State University of New York–Binghamton, and the University of Pennsylvania. He has been a visiting research fellow at the Netherlands Institute for Advanced Study in the Humanities and Social Science, the Harvard Divinity School, and the Weston School of Theology, where he pursued advanced study in theology, ethics, and public policy. He has been the Distinguished Visiting Tinbergen Professor of Social Sciences at Erasmus University in the Netherlands.

Dr. Gawthrop has contributed to numerous volumes on public administration and has written numerous articles on ethics and the administrative implementation of public policy. He is the author of four books: *Bureaucratic Behavior in the Executive Branch; Administrative Politics and Social Change; The Administrative Process and Democratic Theory;* and *Public Sector Management, Systems, and Ethics.* He is coauthor (with Virginia B. Gawthrop) of *Public Administration Review Cumulative Index 1940–1979.* He was editor-in-chief of *Public Administration Review* from 1978 to 1984.